Masterpieces *of* Music
Before 1750

Masterpieces *of* Music
Before 1750

An Anthology of Musical Examples

from Gregorian Chant to J. S. Bach

Compiled and Edited
with Historical and Analytical Notes by
CARL PARRISH *and* JOHN F. OHL

W · W · NORTON & COMPANY · INC · *NEW YORK*

Permission to use material in this book has been granted as follows: Examples 1, 2, 3: *Liber Usualis*, Ed. No. 801, Desclée et Cie., Tournai, 1934. 4: Friedrich Gennrich, *Grundriss einer Formenlehre des mittelälterlichen Liedes*, Max Niemeyer Verlag, Halle, 1932. 5: Denkmäler der Tonkunst in *Osterreich*, 37. Jahrgang, 1. Teil, Gesellschaft zur Herausgabe der Denkmäler der Tonkunst in Oesterreich, Vienna, 1930. 7, 13: H. Besseler, *Die Musik des Mittelalters und der Renaissance*, Potsdamer Verlagsgesellschaft, Produktionsgruppe Akademische Verlagsgesellschaft Athenaion, 1931. 8: G. Adler, *Handbuch der Musikgeschichte*, Max Hesses Verlag, Berlin. 11: Higini Angles, El Codex Musical de las Huelgas, Vol. III, Institut d' Estudie Catalans: Biblioteea de Catalunya, Barcelona, 1931. 12: Johannes Wolf, "Die Tänze des Mittelalters," *Archiv für Musikwissenschaft*, Jahrgang I, 1918–19, Breitkopf & Härtel, Leipzig. 14: Leonard Ellinwood, *Francesco Landini*, Mediaeval Academy of America, 1939. 15: Albert Smijers, *Algemeene muziekgeschiedenis*, Uitgeversmaatschappij W. de Haan N. V., Utrecht, 1938. 17: Johannes Ockeghem, *Collected Works*, Vol. II, Dragan Plamenac, etc., American Musicological Society, 1947. 19: Josquin des Prez, *Werke*, Vol. I, G. Alsbach, Amsterdam. Supplementary chant from *Liber Usualis*, Ed. No. 801, Desclée et Cie., Tournai, 1934. 22: Wilhelm Tappert, *Sang und Klang aus alter Zeit*, Leo Liepmannssohn's Antiquariat, Berlin, 1906. 24: Supplementary chant from *Liber Usualis*, Ed. No. 801, Desclée et Cie., Tournai, 1934. 25: *Tudor Church Music*, Vol. 7, Oxford University Press, London, 1927. 26: Manuscript collection in the possession of Lawrence K. J. Feininger, Collegio Capranica, Rome. 27: Luca Marenzio, *Sämtliche Werke*, Band II, in Publikationen Alterer Musik, Jahrgang 6, Breitkopf & Härtel, Leipzig, 1931. 29: *The Fitzwilliam Virginal Book*, Vol. II, Breitkopf & Härtel, Leipzig, 1899. 35: *Denkmäler der Tonkunst in Osterreich*, Jahrgang 6, 2. Teil, Artaria Verlag, Vienna, 1899. 38: *The Works of Henry Purcell*, Purcell Society Edition, Vol. 6, Novello & Co., Ltd., London, 1895. 41: *Castor et Pollux*, A. Chapuis, ed., Durand & Cie., Paris, 1903. 44: *Georg Friedrich Händel's Werke* (Deutsche Händelgesellschaft), Vol. 58, Leipzig, 1896.

SBN 393 09739 0

1 2 3 4 5 6 7 8 9

O

Contents

Foreword

Summary

Masterpieces of Music Before 1750 is a collection of musical examples
that illustrate the general course of musical style from the early Middle
Ages to the middle of the eighteenth century, selected, arranged, and
edited with a view to their being worked with by the student of the
history of music. Every detail of editorial procedure has had as its objec-
tive the furtherance of this practical purpose. No effort has been spared
to arrive at a method of presentation of the musical text that would make
it useful for analysis in or out of the classroom. Moreover, this music can
be used for actual performance. The detailed account of editorial procedure given below will make clear the specific considerations that have
governed the way the materials have been presented. It should be re-
marked, however, that the selection of each example has been deter-
mined, first of all, by the basic requirement that it be in itself an interesting and beautiful piece of music, well worth performing for the sheer
musical enjoyment it can give, aside from any pedagogical purpose. To
this end, complete compositions or sections of compositions which form
complete musical entities have been used so far as possible.
While the collection makes no pretense to completeness, it is a
repertory of basic musical materials designed to fit the needs of the
beginning student of the history of music, though it is likely that the collection will not be without value to the student who is fairly advanced
in historical studies. It is suggested that the reader make a detailed analysis of each example, writing directly on the music itself, since it is only
by such detailed study that a true understanding of musical styles can be
acquired. Moreover, the collection furnishes what is necessary for the
practical performance of the most characteristic forms and styles in the
periods where adequate illustrative material is often hard to come by.
The purpose of the notes accompanying each example is to indicate the

place that the composition occupies in the history of music, and to suggest
lines upon which an analysis of the music may be undertaken. They
are not intended to supply all the background necessary to an understanding of the example. It is assumed that extensive supplementary reading in standard texts on the history of music will be pursued. The material
in this volume may be advantageously supplemented with further examples, which may be found in available collections such as those of
Schering (*Geschichte der Musik in Beispielen*), Davison-Apel (*Historical Anthology of Music*), Wolf (*Music of Earlier Times*), and Einstein (*A Short History of Music*), as well as in collections of a more
specialized nature.

Full details concerning sources are given in the notes. Where no
specific credit is given for the modern version of an example, it is the
work of the present editors. Where a secondary source has been employed, care has been taken to see to it that the edition used is one whose
authority is generally recognized. Students will through these references
become familiar with the names of some of the important manuscripts
and printed sources of music of the periods treated, and of some of the
basic modern editions of music before 1750. Advanced students may
consult the sources themselves, where available, for additional examples.

Above all, it is the earnest hope of the editors that every example here
given will be performed in whatever manner the circumstances permit,
for it is only through bringing to life in actual sound the music which is
the subject of historical study that musical, artistic and spiritual understanding can be fully achieved.

EDITORIAL PROCEDURE

SHORT SCORE.   Each example is so printed as to facilitate its study at the
piano by a student not able to deal readily with open score. More than
two staves are employed only where fullness of texture precludes the
clear presentation of the material on two. Every example is the complete
musical text of the composition, not a "piano arrangement." Details of
scoring, including orchestration, are indicated in the music itself. Where
a continuo is present the figuring appears in full, as in the original. The
extent to which it is realized depends upon individual circumstances; all
realizations are distinguished from the original text by being given in

small notes. It will thus be clear that in every case the original score can be reconstituted from the version here given.

TEXT IN VOCAL EXAMPLES. In all vocal compositions a complete text for every voice part is given in the music, thus enabling the music to be performed by voices even though printed in short score. All non-English texts other than liturgical Latin have been translated into English that fits the music and can be sung, and this translation is given in the music. These English versions make no pretense to literary distinction, but aim only at giving the sense of the original text as accurately as is consistent with their fitting the music smoothly. There is thus no attempt at preserving rhymes. Liturgical Latin texts are untranslated in the music, an English translation not intended for singing being given at the head of the note. Where the text is Biblical the language of the King James Version or of the Book of Common Prayer is used. Since liturgical Latin is in active use today, both in the Roman Catholic Church and in performances of sacred music by leading choral societies, it has seemed well to use only that language in these instances. All translations are the work of the present editors except as noted.

CLEFS. Only treble and bass clefs are used. When the range of the part concerned is that of the vocal tenor a treble clef with subscript *8* is employed to indicate notes sounding an octave below the normal treble clef.

TRANSPOSITION. Where the example has been transposed to render it more suitable for modern performance, the interval of transposition is indicated at the head of the music.

NOTE VALUES. Any reduction in the original note values for purposes of easier reading is indicated at the head of the example; where there is no such indication there has been no change.

ACCIDENTALS. An accidental above the note to which it refers is a conjecture of the present editors, and may be freely disregarded by anyone who disagrees with its employment. Accidentals in parentheses are precautionary only. All other accidentals are original.

BARRING. In all music originally without bar lines the barring is the work of the present editors, with a few exceptions where it is that of the editor of the modern source. It should be made clear that all modern barring of music that was originally without bars is essentially arbitrary. In every example except those which are unbarred every fifth bar is numbered for ease of reference in discussion and written analysis.

NOTATION OF GREGORIAN CHANT. The method of transcription into modern notation employed in the examples of Gregorian chant is an adaptation by the present editors of that used in the Solesmes editions in modern notation. The chief difference lies in the use of a dotted tie to indicate that repeated notes are to be sung as one, instead of their being written as a single longer note.

ACKNOWLEDGMENTS

The editors are deeply grateful to the many persons whose help has lightened their task, and whose encouragement has made their labors pleasant. The final form of the book owes much to the learned and thoughtful advice of Dr. Paul H. Lang. The transcriptions of Examples 9 and 10 benefited from the assistance of Dr. Gwynn McPeek, who made his own versions available for comparison. The inclusion of Example 26 was made possible by Dr. Thomas McCoughtry Judson, Curator of the Cicognara Collection at the Vatican, who placed a microfilm of the original manuscript owned by Father Feininger at the editors' disposal.

Dr. Alfred Einstein's friendly interest in the book's progress, as well as his help on many practical matters, has placed the editors under a deep obligation which they are happy to acknowledge. He generously allowed the use of his own manuscript copies from the original editions of Examples 20 and 21, and suggested the selection of Example 22. Most important of all, his reading of the completed book in proof was an act of kindness for which the editors cannot sufficiently express their gratitude.

Finally, the editors wish to thank their many friends and colleagues for valuable suggestions on details of editing and translation, and for their continuous interest and encouragement; and to thank Addison Burnham and Robert Farlow, of W. W. Norton & Company, Inc., for their consistent helpfulness and understanding during the whole process of the book's production.

Carl Parrish
John F. Ohl

Masterpieces *of* Music

Before 1750

1. Gregorian Chant
Antiphon, *Laus Deo Patri*, and
Psalm 113, *Laudate pueri*

FOR SECOND VESPERS, FEAST OF THE HOLY TRINITY

Ant. Let praise resound from our mouths to God the Father, and to the Son, His equal, and to Thee, Holy Spirit, with unceasing zeal, through all eternity.

Ps. 1. Praise the Lord, ye servants: O praise the Name of the Lord.

2. Blessed be the Name of the Lord: from this time forth for evermore.

3. The Lord's Name is praised: from the rising up of the sun unto the going down of the same.

4. The Lord is high above all heathen; and his glory above the heavens.

5. Who is like unto the Lord our God, that hath his dwelling so high; and yet humbleth himself to behold the things that are in heaven and earth!

6. He taketh up the simple out of the dust: and lifteth the poor out of the mire:

7. That he may set him with the princes: even with the princes of his people.

8. He maketh the barren woman to keep house: and to be a joyful mother of children.

9. Glory be to the Father, and to the Son: and to the Holy Ghost;

10. As it was in the beginning, is now, and ever shall be: world without end. Amen.

Gregorian chant is purely melodic, one-line (monophonic) music; hence its other common name—plainsong. Its rhythm is free and irregular, corresponding to the natural accents of the text; thus the note values of editions in modern notation, such as the present example, are not intended to indicate precise durations. The classification and organization of the chants rest on a system of melodic formulas and scale relationships known as the eight *church modes*. The melodies fall into three main classes: *syllabic*, with one note to each syllable; *neumatic*, with groups of two to four notes to a syllable predominating (represented by *neumes* in the original notation); and *melismatic*, with still longer groups of notes to single syllables. When, as in the services of the Office, a whole Psalm is performed, it is chanted in simple syllabic style to a *Psalm tone*. The greater part of each verse of the Psalm is intoned on a single reciting note (the *tenor*), the opening of the first verse employing a simple melodic formula, and the mid-point and close of each verse being marked by a similar melodic rise and fall. There are eight Psalm tones, corresponding to the eight modes, so that the *antiphon* (see below) and Psalm tone are tonally connected. There is also an exceptional tone, called *tonus peregrinus*, which has two different reciting notes. In earliest times the two balancing parts of each verse of the Psalm were chanted antiphonally between two choruses. Later, a refrain, called the antiphon, was sung after each pair of verses. Nowadays on important festivals the antiphon is sung at the beginning of the Psalm and is repeated at the end after the *Gloria Patri*, which is always sung after the Psalm itself. On less important occasions only the first phrase of the antiphon is sung before the Psalm. The performance alternates between solo and chorus. Most antiphons are in syllabic style, but those for the greater feasts, like the present example, are often neumatic. (For a purely syllabic antiphon see the example given on page 90.)

Source: *Liber usualis* (Edition No. 801), Tournai, 1934; Antiphon, p. 914; Psalm, p. 150.

1. Gregorian Chant
Antiphon, *Laus Deo Patri*
Psalm 113, *Laudate pueri*

Mode 4 (Hypophrygian)

[Solo]   [Chorus]

Laus_____ De____o__ Pa - tri, * pa - ri_____li - que__ Pro - li,

et ti - bi__ San____cte stu - di - o per____en____ni__ Spi____ri____tus,

no - stro__ re____so - net ab__ o_____re om__ne per__ ae - vum.

Tone 4

[Solo]   [Chorus]

1. Lau - da_____te pu - er - i Do - mi - num: * lau - da - te no - men Do - mi__ni.

2. Sit nomen Domini _ . . . . be - ne - di - ctum,
3. A solis ortu usque _ . . . . ad oc - ca - sum,
4. Excelsus super omnes . . . . gen - tes Do - mi - nus,
5. Quis sicut Dominus Deus noster, qui in _ . . . . . al - tis ha - bi - tat,
6. Suscitans a _ . . . . ter - ra in - o - pem,
7. Ut collocet eum _ . . . . cum prin - ci - pi - bus,
8. Qui habitare facit steri - _ . . . . lem in do - mo,
9. Gloria Pa - . _ . . . . tri, et Fi - li - o,
10. Sicut erat in principio, et . . . . nunc, et sem - per,

(2.)* ex hoc nunc, et _ . . . . us - que in__ sae - cu__lum.
(3.)* laudabi - . _ . . . . le no - men__ Do - mi - ni.
(4.)* et super caelos _ . . . . glo - ri - a e__jus.
(5.)* et humilia respicit in cae - . _ . . . . lo et in__ ter____ra?
(6.)* et de stercore _ . . . . e - ri - gens__ pau - pe____ram.
(7.)* cum principibus _ . . . . po - pu - li__ su____i.
(8.)* matrem fili - . _ . . . . o - rum lae__ tan____tem.
(9.)* et Spi - . _ . . . . ri - tu - i San____cto.
(10.)* et in saecula sae - . _ . . . . cu - lo - rum.__ A____men.

Chorus: Laus Deo, [etc., as above]

2. Gregorian Chant
Alleluia, *Vidimus stellam*

FROM THE MASS FOR EPIPHANY

Alleluia. We have seen His star in the East,
and are come with gifts to worship the Lord.
Alleluia.

Those sections of the text of the Mass that are invariable throughout the church year—Kyrie, Gloria, Credo, Sanctus, Agnus Dei—are referred to as the *Ordinary* of the Mass. The *Alleluia* belongs to that group of chants of the Mass which is called the *Proper*, because the texts of these chants change according to the church season, or the occasion commemorated. The Alleluia is always in a highly melismatic style, this being particularly noticeable in the setting of the word "alleluia" itself, which concludes with a long and elaborate melisma on the final syllable, called the *jubilus* because of its joyful character. It was through the practice of adding text to this melisma that the *sequence* arose.* The text of the *versicle* which follows is appropriate to the day for which the chant is intended, and its setting is usually less consistently melismatic. The formal organization of most Alleluias is rather complex because, in addition to the repetition of whole sections, motives from the Alleluia are used in the versicle, together with new material. The alternation of solo and chorus, and the repetition of sections in performance, are indicated in the example.

Source: *Liber usualis* (Edition No. 801), Tournai, 1934, p. 460.

* Concerning the sequence see p. 8.
Note: The sign beneath the third note from the end of the first chorus phrase denotes the *quilisma*; it is thought that it indicated a slight *vibrato* on the note in question.

2. Gregorian Chant

Alleluia, *Vidimus stellam*

Mode 2 (Hypodorian)

[Solo] Al - le - lu - ia [Chorus] ✶ Al - le - lu - ia

[Solo] ℣ Vi - di - mus stel - lam e - jus in O - ri - en - te et ve - ni - mus cum mu - ne - ri - bus ad - o - ra - re [Chorus] ✶ Do - mi - num [Solo] Al - le - lu - ia [Chorus] (a)

3. Gregorian Chant
Sequence, *Victimae Paschali*

1. Christians, to the Paschal Victim offer your thankful praises.
2. The Lamb the sheep hath ransomed: Christ, by sin undefiled, reconcileth sinners to the Father.
3. Death and Life in a conflict sore and wondrous contended: Life's Captain, he that died, deathless reigneth.
4. Speak, Mary, declaring, what thou sawest wayfaring?
5. His tomb, who passed through its portal, His glory, who rose from death immortal:
6. Bright angels attesting, the shroud and napkin resting,
7. The Lord, my hope, hath arisen: to Galilee He goeth before you.
8. We know that Christ is risen henceforth ever living: have mercy, Victor King, pardon giving.

The *sequence* is the earliest and most important type of trope.* It was the result of a practice adopted by a ninth-century monk, Notker Balbulus, who added texts to the long melisma (*jubilus*) at the end of the Alleluia, to facilitate the memorizing of these long textless melodies. The practice of adding text to a pre-existing melody soon gave way to that of creating independent compositions, whose typical poetic and musical form is illustrated by this example. It consisted of a number of two-line versicles, varying in length, usually in unrhymed prose, the whole often being introduced and concluded by a single, unpaired versicle. Sequences continued to be composed through the thirteenth century, those of the later period being more strictly metrical, and even hymnlike. Of the five

* The trope is explained on p. 18.

sequences in use at the present day, this example, attributed to the monk Wipo of Burgundy (eleventh century), is the only one in the typical early form. An instrumental counterpart of the sequence is the *estampie* (see page 33). The opening of another early sequence is shown on page 17.

Source: *Liber usualis* (Edition No. 801), Tournai, 1934, p. 780. English translation from: Cook, *The Use of Plainsong*, Nashdom Abbey, 1928, p. 24.

3. Gregorian Chant
Sequence, *Victimae Paschali* (11th c.)

Mode I (Dorian)

[Solo]　　　　　　　　　　　　　　　[Chorus]

1. Vi - cti - mae pa - scha - li　lau - des　　im - mo - lent Chri - sti - a - ni.

2. A - gnus red - e - mit　o - ves:　　Chri - stus　in - no - cens　Pa - tri
3. Mors et　vi - ta　du - el - lo　　con - fli - xe - re　mi - ran - do:

re - con - ci - li - a - vit　pec - ca - to - res.　4. Dic　no - bis　Ma -
dux　vi - tae mor - tu - us　re - gnat vi - vus.　6. An - ge - li - cos

ri - a,_____ quid vi - di - sti　in　vi - a?　5. Se - pul - crum
tes - tes,_____ su - da - ri - um,　et　ves - tes,　7. Sur - re - xit

Chri - sti　vi - ven_____tis,　et　glo - ri - am vi - di　re -
Chri - stus spes me_____a:　prae - ce - det　su - os　in　Ga -

sur - gen_____tis:　　8. Sci - mus Chri - stum sur - re - xis - se
li - lae_____am.

a　mor - tu - is　ve - re:　tu　no - bis,　vic - tor Rex,

mi - se - re_____re.　A_____men._____ Al - le - lu_____ia.

4. Trouvère Song
Virelai, *Or la truix*

Monophonic secular music of the Middle Ages is represented principally by the lyrical melodies of the knightly *troubadours* and *trouvères* of the twelfth and thirteenth centuries. Nearly 1,700 of these melodies are extant, which are notated as music of a single line. Contemporaneous pictures usually show the singers of these melodies with an instrument which, it is thought, was restricted to brief improvisatory introductions, interludes, and postludes. These songs usually lie within the compass of an octave, and many are in the church modes, especially Dorian and Mixolydian, although a great many are in major (like *Or la truix*) and minor. Most of the songs have no indication of rhythm; modern transcribers have usually fitted them into one or another of the six *rhythmic modes*, according to the text. The rhythmic modes are a system of metrical patterns derived from classical Latin and Greek poetry, whose alternation of long and short note values is such that triple time in various forms usually results. The present example is in the first rhythmic mode (*trochaic*). Trouvère songs are distinguished from those of the troubadours by more clearly defined rhythm and formal structure, also by a greater variety of forms. The principal forms used by the trouvères were the *ballade, rondeau,* and *virelai*. Example 4 is a *virelai*, consisting of a refrain, followed by a new phrase, which is then repeated with new words; the music of the refrain then follows, with new text, and the whole ends with a repetition of the refrain with its original words.* Thus the verse pattern is *ab cd ef ab*, while the musical pattern is *ab cc ab ab*.

* A special interest is attached to Example 4 in that it is one of several such songs that have come down to us as the tenor of a thirteenth-century motet. (This motet can be found in Gennrich, *Rondeaux, Virelais und Balladen*, Göttingen, 1927, Vol. 2, p. 320; also, in a slightly different version, in Rokseth, *Polyphonies du XIIIe siècle*, Vol. 3, p. 173.)

Sources: Oxford, Bodleian, Douce 308, fol. 226 and 237; also Montpellier, Faculté de Médecine, H 196, fol. 338.

Transcription: Gennrich, *Grundriss einer Formenlehre des Mittelalterlichen Liedes*, Halle, 1932, p. 72.

4. Trouvère Song (12th–13th c.)
Virelai, *Or la truix*

5. Neidhart von Reuenthal
Minnelied, *Willekommen Mayenschein*

An outpouring of lyrical secular melody similar to that of the troubadours and trouvères occurred contemporaneously and somewhat later in the songs of the German Minnesinger. The music of these Teutonic knight-poets shows a considerable influence of the troubadours, but is distinguished from the latter in several important respects, both musical and literary. The word "Minne" means "love," but Minnelieder texts tend toward the narrative rather than the amorous, and many are of a religious nature. Since German verse of the period was governed by accent rather than by length of syllables, the rhythmic modes are not applicable to the Minnelieder, which are usually transcribed by modern scholars in binary or ternary rhythms, according to the number of strong accents of the poem. The notation of the present example is an adaptation of the transcription of Wolfgang Schmieder, dotted bar lines being used to indicate rhythmic groupings, and solid bars drawn part way through the stave indicating ends of lines. A short horizontal line above a note indicates a prolongation and a pause. It will be seen that the resulting rhythm is duple. The Minnesinger employed the church modes more frequently than did the troubadours and trouvères. The musical form most frequently employed by the Minnesinger was the *Bar*, which consisted of two *Stollen* (stanzas) and an *Abgesang* (conclusion), forming the scheme *aab*. Another form was the *Leich* (the *lai* of the trouvères), which was closely related to the sequence with its double versicles.* Example 5 is by Neidhart von Reuenthal, a Minnesinger who lived in the first half of the thirteenth century, and whose songs often suggest the character of folk art. It is in the typical *Barform*, with two *Stollen*, each with a different text, and an

* Concerning the sequence see p. 8.

Abgesang. A feature of its musical structure which is found in many Minnelieder is the similar ending of *Stollen* and *Abgesang.*

Source: Berlin MS: germ. fol. 779, c, 11, Bl. 141a.
          Facsimile: *DTOe* 37, 1, Vienna, 1930, p. 4.
          Transcription: *DTOe* 37, 1, p. 31.

5. Neidhart von Reuenthal (13th c.)
Minnelied, *Willekommen Mayenschein*

Wil - le - ko - men may - en - schein | wer mocht vns er -
Wel - come art thou, May's bright sun, who could make us

ge - czen dein | wann du kanst ver - swen - den pein | das
thee for - get? For thou canst our ills ex - pel, as

sagt uns die - se diett | Win - ter der ist hie ge - legen
ev - ry - one doth say. Win - ter has so long here lain,

auff dem velde vnd in den wegen | wil - lig - lich gab
on the fields and in the paths; that he fain would

er den segen | da er von hyn - nen schiett | Nun wil - tu die
bless us all and hence from here de - part. Now wilt thou the

hai - de a - ber e - ren | und wilt klei - ne vo - ge - lein dein
wood - land fill with blos - som; and wilt teach the lit - tle birds thy

sus - se sti - me le____ren | das sie in dem
mel - o - dies so love____ly, so that all the

wal - de | pal - de | im sus - se sank ge - me - ren.
woods and mea - dows will ring with their sweet sing - ing.

6. Parallel Organum
Sequence, *Rex caeli, Domine*

1. King of the Heavens, Lord of the wave-sounding sea,
2. Of the shining sun and of the squalid earth,
3. Thy humble servants, venerating Thee with pious accents
4. Entreat Thee that Thou wilt order them freed from mani-
fold ills.

The earliest type of polyphonic music was called *organum*. In its sim-
plest form it consisted in adding to a Gregorian melody a second, or
organal voice which exactly paralleled the original plainsong at the interval of a fifth or fourth above or below, both these lines often being
doubled in the octave. The next step beyond this mechanical paralleling
of voices occurred during the ninth and tenth centuries, and is illustrated
in the present example. This shows the opening of an early sequence.
(Note that the typical single verse which normally precedes the sets of
double versicles is lacking.) To the original melody in the upper voice has
been added a lower part, which moves for the most part in parallel fourths
with the original plainsong, except at the beginning and end of each line.
At these points it moves from and returns to the unison. This example
comes from a famous theoretical treatise of the ninth century, the *Musica
enchiriadis* (*Musical Handbook*), which contains the first written discussion of polyphony. It was formerly attributed to the monk Hucbald
(c. 840–930), whose authorship is now disputed.

Source: M. Gerbert, *Scriptores*, St. Blaise, 1784, Vol. I, p. 167.

6. Parallel Organum (9th c.)
Sequence, *Rex caeli, Domine*

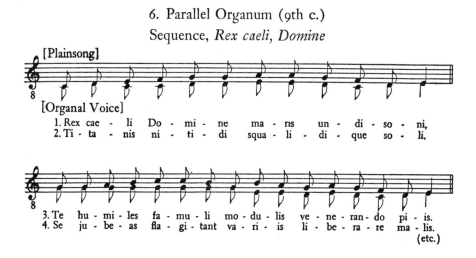

[Plainsong]

[Organal Voice]

1. Rex cae - li Do - mi - ne ma - ris un - di - so - ni,
2. Ti - ta - nis ni - ti - di squa - li - di - que so - li.

3. Te hu - mi - les fa - mu - li mo - du - lis ve - ne - ran - do pi - is.
4. Se ju - be - as fla - gi - tant va - ri - is li - be - ra - re ma - lis.

(etc.)

7. Free Organum
Trope, *Agnus Dei*

O Lamb of God, who takest away the sins of the world,
Who art made holy, that Thou mayest purify the acts
    of human kind,
Have mercy upon us.

After the rather definite codification of the whole repertory of Gregorian chant in the sixth to eighth centuries, the most important new chant melodies composed were of the sort known as *tropes*, which were written in great numbers from the ninth to the thirteenth century. These were amplifying or explanatory phrases interpolated in the recognized liturgical text. At first, the new words were made to fit the notes of a section of the original chant; the most important manifestation of this sort of trope was the sequence.* Later, all tropes, including sequences, were set to newly composed music. In this example, which comes from the twelfth century, the trope is an insertion in the first part of an Agnus Dei. This is a trope in two-part free organum. Rhythmically it is similar to plainsong in its irregularity and free flow. But instead of the more or less rigid parallel motion of the earlier organum (as in Example 6), contrary motion is predominant. The harmonic intervals between the voices are chiefly those regarded by early theorists as consonances—octaves, fifths, fourths, and unisons; but there are also a number of thirds, regarded at this period as dissonances, and at the cadence of the trope several thirds are used in succession, an unusual feature at this time. (The example follows the transcription of Besseler; for a quite different interpretation see Wooldridge, *Early English Harmony*, Vol. II, London, 1913, page 56.)

* Examples of the sequence are on p. 10 and p. 17.

18

Source: Cambridge Univ. Lib. MS Ff. I. 17.
    Facsimile: Wooldridge, *Early English Harmony*, Vol. I, London,
    1897, Plate 27.
    Transcription: Besseler, *Die Musik des Mittelalters*, Potsdam, 1931,
    p. 95.

7. Free Organum (12th c.)
Trope, *Agnus Dei*

8. Melismatic Organum
School of St. Martial, *Benedicamus Domino*

Let us bless the Lord.

The Abbey of St. Martial at Limoges, in southern France, was the location of an important school that figures prominently in the development of organum during the years from about 1100 to 1150, preceding the more famous school of Notre Dame in the north.* In the St. Martial style, the lower voice, or *tenor*, utilizes a phrase of Gregorian chant, each note of which is greatly prolonged, while the upper (organal) voice puts elaborate melismas in free rhythm against each tenor note. At the point where each tenor note begins, the two voices form intervals of a unison, fourth, fifth, or octave; between these points the tenor note behaves in the manner of a pedal point against the upper voice, which moves freely over consonant and dissonant notes at will. The chant upon which this example is based is sung at the conclusion of the Mass. Only the beginning of the organum is given.

Source: Paris Bibl. Nat. lat. 3719, fol. 70.
        Transcription: F. Ludwig, in: G. Adler, *Handbuch der Musik-geschichte*, Frankfurt am Main, 1924, p. 148.

  * Concerning the Notre Dame school see p. 22.

8. Melismatic Organum
School of St. Martial, *Benedicamus Domino*

(etc.)

9. Perotin
Organum, *Alleluya* (*Nativitas*)

FOR SECOND VESPERS, FEAST OF THE NATIVITY OF THE BLESSED VIRGIN MARY

The *Alleluya* addition to the antiphon versicle *Nativitas* is a characteristic organum of the Notre Dame school of composition. The Parisian cathedral became the center of musical development around the middle of the twelfth century, when the outstanding composer of such pieces was Leonin. Under his successor, Perotin, the school maintained its dominant position throughout the thirteenth century. The work of the school is concentrated in the *Magnus liber organi* (*The Great Book of Organa*). Perotin, who is thought to have commenced his activities at the cathedral about 1183, contributed many conductus and organa in 2, 3, and 4 parts to the Notre Dame repertory. The example given has features of both organum (unmeasured) and discant (measured) styles, as it begins in an unmeasured manner but later (bar 33) takes on a measured character. In the former the two upper voices are in the third rhythmic mode (*dactylic*), while the tenor is unmeasured; the passages in discant have modal rhythm in all the parts.* The section given is that which framed the antiphon versicles. In liturgical performance the *Alleluya* was sung by soloists, and was followed by the original Gregorian Alleluia (given at the end of this example) that forms the tenor of the organum, which was sung by the whole choir. After this came a versicle sung by soloists in three-part organum style similar to that of the *Alleluya*, followed by the choral rendition of another plainchant versicle; finally the *Alleluya* organum was repeated by the soloists. The principal features of the Notre Dame technique are represented in this example. The two

---

* The rhythmic modes are briefly described on p. 11.

upper voices are equal in range, and cross frequently. They have phrases of varying lengths, and it will be noted that they sometimes outline triads (as in bar 26 of the upper part, and bar 39 of the lower), and occasionally move in parallel fifths (bars 4, 8, 15) and fourths (bars 2, 23, 30, 51). Contrary to principles stated by theorists of the period, this organum does not begin consonantly, the upper voice forming a sort of appoggiatura with the tenor. Possibly this was avoided in actual performance by delaying slightly the entrance of the tenor. It is interesting to note that all the organa and conductus of the Notre Dame school are notated "in score," a practice that was discarded about 1225 and did not reappear until the latter sixteenth century.

Source: Montpellier, Faculté de Médecine, H 196, fol. 145, 146.
Facsimile: Y. Rokseth, *Polyphonies du XIIIe siècle*, Vol. I, Paris, 1935.
Slightly different versions of this organum may be found in Y. Rokseth, *op. cit.*, Vol. II, p. 16, and in *Die drei- und vierstimmigen Notre-Dame-Organa* (Publikationen älterer Musik, 11, ed. by Heinrich Husmann), Leipzig, 1940, p. 86.

9. Perotin (12th c.)
Organum, *Alleluya* (*Nativitas*)

Gregorian form of the *Alleluya* tenor

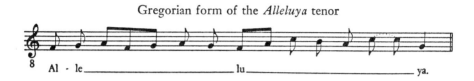

Al - le_____ lu _____ ya.

10. Motet

School of Notre Dame

En non Diu! Quant voi; Eius in Oriente

Of the various forms of composition practiced by the great school of musical composition at Notre Dame in Paris in the twelfth and thirteenth centuries, the most important was the *motet.* Unlike the organum of the period, its rhythm was rigidly organized throughout by use of the rhythmic modes. In writing a motet, the thirteenth-century composer took for his tenor, or lowest voice, part of a melismatic passage of Gregorian chant, which he first put into one of the rhythmic modes. The source of the plainsong was indicated in the manuscripts by the first few words of its original text (*incipit*). The words attached to the tenor of this example show that its source is that part of the versicle of the Alleluia shown in Example 2 which commences with the words "eius in oriente." * The tenor as a whole lacks text, and was presumably performed by instruments. A second voice, with text, and therefore called *motetus* (having words—the source of the name of the whole form) or *duplum* (second voice), was then invented by the composer, and fitted to the tenor in such a way as to form consonances (unison, fourth, fifth, octave) at strongly accented points. Between these accents, any other intervals, no matter how dissonant, were allowed. Most commonly a third voice, the *triplum*, was then added to the tenor according to the same principles, no account, however, being taken of any clashes it might form with the motetus. The earlier practice was to employ Latin tropes of the tenor chant for the texts of the upper voices, but gradually

* The composer has employed two sections of the melisma, repeating each, the first serving as the basis for the first half of his composition, the second for the last half.

all connection between the original chant text and the sentiments expressed in the upper voices was lost. At the height of the development of the motet, French and Provençal texts, often of a wholly secular nature, were regularly employed. This tendency toward secularization reached its climax with the use of secular tunes as tenors (Example 4 was so employed). In the present late thirteenth-century example, the texts are love songs, the opening triplum phrase, repeated by the motetus at the end, being a refrain quoted from a trouvère song. Such a device as the interchange of material between the two upper voices, which can be seen by comparing bars 1–4 with bars 21–24, is a fairly common thirteenth-century device. On the other hand, the use of canon at the unison in the two upper voices in bars 5–8 is exceptional and shows the beginning of later contrapuntal techniques.

Source: Montpellier, Faculté de Médecine, H 196, fol. 145, 146.

Facsimile: Y. Rokseth, *Polyphonies du XIIIe siècle*, Vol. I, Paris, 1935.

For different transcriptions of this motet, see Y. Rokseth, *op. cit.*, Vol. II, p. 205, and J. Wolf, *Handbuch der Notationskunde*, Vol. I, Leipzig, 1913, p. 240.

10. Motet (13th c.)

School of Notre Dame, *En non Diu! Quant voi; Eius in Oriente*

♩=♩. En non Diu! que que___nus di_____e, Quant voi l'her - be_____
Now in truth! what - e'er___ they tell___ us, When the grass is_____

[Triplum]

[Motetus]

Quant voi la___ rose es - pa - ni - e, L'her - be vert et___
When I see___ the ro - ses bud - ding, Gras - ses green and___

[Tenor] EIUS IN ORIENTE

vert___ et le___ tans cler, Et le ro - si - gnol___ chan -
green___ and wea___ther clear, And the night - in - gale___ doth

le___ tans cler, Et le ro - si - gnol___ chan - ter,
wea___ther clear, And the night - in - gale___ doth sing,

ter, A___ donc fine a___ mors___ me pri___e Do - ce -
sing, Then___ my___ dain - ty___ love___ doth beg___ me Sweet - ly

A dont_ fine___ a___mors m'en - vi - e De joi - e fere
Then my_ dain___ty_ love doth beg me To re - joice with

ment___ d'u___ne jo - li - ve - té chan - ter: "Ma - ri -
of___ a___ pret - ty tale of love to sing: "Ma - ri -

et___ me___ner, Car qui n'aime, il___ ne___ vit mi - e;
her___ and_ play, He who loves not___ lives___ not ei - ther;

11. Conductus

De castitatis thalamo

That pure nuptial chamber, a virgin's womb, is the special place provided by the Father for the Son. In all the world, where could one find the like, that could hold the Son, the equal of the Father.

Latin songs of the twelfth and thirteenth centuries which were not derived from plainsong were called *conductus* (plural *conductus*), whether monophonic or polyphonic. The polyphonic conductus was accordingly a piece written on a tenor which itself was a free creation of the composer. A further distinctive feature of the form is the fact that the voices above the tenor are for the most part rhythmically identical with it, so that a note-against-note style results. Modal rhythm is employed, all voices use the same text, and the tenor in this instance is vocal, not instrumental as in Example 10. Harmonies are treated in the same manner as in the motet of the period. In the example here shown, almost no harsh dissonances occur between the accented points. It should be noted, however, that the third was regarded as a dissonance. As in this example, the first and penultimate syllables of the text are usually prolonged over many bars. These passages have at times been thought to be instrumental preludes and postludes to the central vocal section, but it is very much more likely that they were vocalized by the singers. The extended use of harmonic and melodic sequence in the final vocalized passage of this conductus is noteworthy and exceptional.

Source: Codex de Las Huelgas (Monastery of Las Huelgas near Burgos), fol. 131.
Facsimile: H. Anglès, *El Codex musical de las Huelgas*, Vol. II, Barcelona, 1931.
Transcription: *Ibid.*, Vol. III, p. 306.

11. Conductus

De castitatis thalamo

De_____

ca - sti - ta - tis tha - la___mo

Ven - trem vir___gi___na___lem   Pa - ter___ de - dit   Fi - li - o

Va - lem spe___ci - a___lem.   In - ve - ni___re

po___te___rat   Quis in mun - do ta___lem   Ut por - ta - ret

Fi - li - um   Pa - tri co - e - qua___

___lem.

12. Estampie
Instrumental Dance

The *estampie* (also called *stantipes, estampida, stampita,* and *istanpitta*) is a dance of the thirteenth and fourteenth centuries, and one of the oldest forms of instrumental music. The name comes from the Provençal word *estamper,* meaning "to stamp," which may indicate the nature of the dance. Its form may be derived from the vocal sequence, in that it consists of several sections, called *puncta* (singular *punctum*), each of which consists of a statement which is repeated. Unlike the sequence, however, each statement has a different ending, or cadence, the first being called *ouvert* (open), the second *clos* (closed), corresponding to our half and full cadences. In a treatise written about 1300, the theorist Johannes de Grocheo writes that the dance consists of from five to seven *puncta;* those with fewer than five are called *ductia.* The present example, from a thirteenth-century manuscript, is in two voices, and is exceedingly interesting for its treatment of the principal motive, which appears in the lower voice during the first two *puncta,* then in the upper voice, transposed, for the rest of the piece. The motive is slightly varied rhythmically in the last *punctum.* Dance music, with its symmetrical periods and definite cadences, has from earliest times been an important factor in the shaping of instrumental music. The use of different key signatures in the various voices of polyphonic compositions, as in this example, is very common in music written before 1500. In recent times the term "partial signature" has been applied to this practice. For other uses of this system of notation see Examples 14 and 16.

Source: British Museum, Harleian 978.
　　　　Facsimile: Wooldridge, *Early English Harmony,* Vol. I, London, 1897, Plate 19.
　　　　Transcription: Wolf, "Die Tänze des Mittelalters," in *Archiv für Musikwissenschaft,* I (1918–19), p. 20.

12. Estampie (13th c.)
Instrumental Dance

13. Guillaume de Machaut
Agnus Dei (I) from the Mass

O Lamb of God, that takest away the sins of the world,
  have mercy upon us.

The new musical style which was introduced at the beginning of the fourteenth century in France, and slightly later in Italy, is known as the *Ars
nova* (new art) from the title of a treatise by one of its first practitioners,
the French composer and theorist, Phillipe de Vitry. The greatest figure
of the period in France was the composer and poet Guillaume de Machaut,
who wrote both sacred and secular music. In addition to a large number
of motets, and of secular compositions in all the important forms, he was
the composer of the first complete polyphonic setting of the ordinary of
the Mass by a single composer, a type of composition which rapidly became of great importance, and remained so through the sixteenth century.
The music of the French *Ars nova* is more refined and expressive than
that of the preceding period, which was called *Ars antiqua* (old art) by
the exponents of the new style. Modal rhythm disappears, the counterpoint employed is much freer, and the melodic lines more flowing. The
harmonies make more frequent use of the third as a consonance, resulting in an effect more pleasing to modern ears, though there is sometimes
a fair amount of rather violent and, according to later standards, arbitrary dissonance. The cadences have the effect of utilizing two leading
tones, one to the fifth of the chord of resolution as well as one to the
tonic. The motets of Machaut and his contemporaries are usually constructed on a plainsong tenor, the rhythmic and formal organization of
which is based upon an *isorhythmic* principle (iso-: "same"), a fact
which gives rise to the term *isorhythmic motet*. This principle involves

the repetition of both a melodic and a rhythmic pattern, these patterns being so planned that they differ in length, and thus overlap one another. In the present example from his Mass, Machaut employs only the principle of rhythmic repetition, the use of a pattern being extended to all the parts, not confined to the tenor. As a note-by-note comparison will reveal, the tenor and contratenor have isorhythmic passages in bars 8–14 and 15–21; the motetus and triplum in bars 8–11 and 15–18. The example is printed so as to facilitate this comparison. This is a *cantus firmus* composition in which the tenor is taken from Mass VIII of the *Graduale Romanum*. The contratenor, being without text, was probably instrumental.

Source: H. Besseler, *Die Musik des Mittelalters und der Renaissance*, (Bücken, *Handbuch der Musikwissenschaft*), Potsdam, 1931, p. 149 (After F. Ludwig).

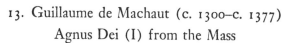

13. Guillaume de Machaut (c. 1300–c. 1377)
Agnus Dei (I) from the Mass

14. Francesco Landini
Ballata, *Chi più le vuol sapere*

The *Ars nova* appeared in Italy of the *trecento* (fourteenth century) somewhat later than in France. Italian music, like Italian literature of this period, shows considerable French influence. However, a more progressive spirit is evident in the natural and spontaneous style of Italian melody, in the tendency of the tenor to function as a support to the top voice, and in the absence of the plainsong *cantus firmus.* Moreover, the French isorhythmic principle is not employed in Italy. Secular music was the chief type cultivated in the brief flowering of the Italian school of the latter fourteenth century, whose outstanding composer was the blind Florentine organist, Francesco Landini. The forms used by him were the *madrigal, ballata* and *caccia.* The ballata, derived from the French virelai,* had now lost its original dancelike character and become stylized in its polyphonic treatment by Italian composers. There are 87 two-voiced and 49 three-voiced ballatas by Landini, some of which are longer and more melismatic than this example. The close of this piece illustrates the so-called "Landini cadence," in which the upper voice moves from the seventh degree to the tone below, and then leaps to the tonic. This cadence was not peculiar to Landini, but was employed by most *Ars nova* composers. Like Examples 12 and 16 this composition has a "partial signature."

Source: MS Florence, Bibl. Medicea Laurenziana, Pal. 87 ("Squarcialupi Codex").
Transcription: Ellinwood: *The Works of Francesco Landini*, Cambridge, 1939, p. 52.

* For a description of the virelai see p. 11.

14. Francesco Landini (1325–1397)

Ballata, *Chi più le vuol sapere*

[Note values quartered]

1. 5. Chi___ più___ le vuol sa___pe___re; quel___
   5 Who___ wi___shes to know___ them___ more, will___
   4. Chè___ ra___do'un dol - ce___ ca___so, tor___
   For___ sel___dom will hap___py___ for - tune___

men'___ le___ sa,___ 2. Co - lui sa po___co'l
know___ them___ less,___ And he knows lit___tle
___ ne___ rà. 3. Dun - que stol - to è qual
___ re___ turn.___ Then fool - ish in___deed

qual cre - de___po - te___re Al___cun
of them who___ i - ma___gines that___ he
buon ve - de'l___ pia - ce___re Et___ nol
is he who___plea-sure___ sees and___ takes

bo___chon___ a - ver gian - mai per - fec___
e___ver___ will have one that is per___
pren___de,___ per di - re'il vo' più net___
it___ not, say - ing he will do bet___

to.

fect.

to.

ter.

15. Guillaume Dufay
Kyrie (I) from the Mass "Se la face ay pale"

Lord, have mercy on us.

Guillaume Dufay is the outstanding figure in the Burgundian school of composers that flourished in the first half of the fifteenth century, and which established the compositional techniques that led to the great flowering of vocal polyphony in the period of Lassus and Palestrina. Dufay's works show a remarkable diversity in style between his early and late periods, the former maintaining a good deal of Machaut's dry angularity and use of arbitrary discord, while the later compositions exhibit great refinement and technical mastery. This change seems to have occurred after Dufay had become acquainted with the techniques of imitation and *faux bourdon* (consecutive chords of the sixth) introduced by his great English contemporary, Dunstable. The great period of Mass composition begins with Dufay, who was one of the first composers to employ secular tunes as *cantus firmi* for such works. There are Masses by him on the two tunes that were most used by composers in the fifteenth and sixteenth centuries—"L'homme armé," and "Se la face ay pale." Such tunes were usually confined to the tenor, and were used in long notes, as in this example. Only the first half of the tune is used in this movement. The Christe which follows is a free composition without a *cantus firmus*, while the second Kyrie employs the second half of the tune. The tune itself as it appears in Dufay's chanson is given at the end of the example; the textless melisma at the end of the tune was probably performed by an instrument. Unlike the predominantly vocal medium of the *a cappella* period of the sixteenth century, the ensemble of Dufay's time always included instruments. Chapel musicians of the Burgundian

43

court at Dijon included players on the organ, recorder, oboe and viol. In sacred music, instruments probably doubled voice parts, although they may have been confined to the wordless interludes.* The individual instrumental lines are thought to have been sharply distinct in tone color, and it is generally believed that expressive nuances were not employed.

Source: Trent, Codex 88; Sistine Chapel Lib., 14, 25.
      Transcription: Smijers: *Algemeene Muziek Geschiedenis,* Utrecht, 1938, p. 101.
Source of "Se la face ay pale": Oxford, Bodleian, Canonici Misc. 213
      Transcription: Stainer, *Early Bodleian Music,* London, 1898, p. 140.

---

* The precise manner of fitting the text syllables to the notes is a matter of conjecture all through the fifteenth century and through the earlier part of the sixteenth. Manuscripts and printed editions of the period give only general indications, leaving it to the singer to decide the details of how the syllables should be placed. In the present example, the underlaying of the text is that of A. Smijers, who has interpreted the tenor as being instrumental, and has therefore not added words. For a quite different underlaying of the words of this piece see DTOe, VII, p. 120.

15. Guillaume Dufay (c. 1400–1474)
Kyrie (I) from the Mass "Se la face ay pale"

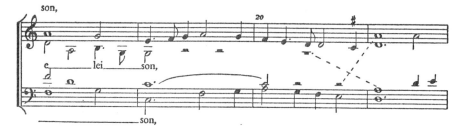

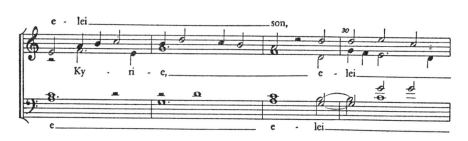

The tune "Se la face ay pale" (Tenor of Dufay's chanson on the tune)

[Note values halved]

Se la face ay pa——le, la cause est a-mer,
If my face is pal——lid, know the cause is love,

C'est la prin-ci-pa——le, et tant m'est a-mer a-mer—— qu'en la mer me
It a-lone doth cause—— it, and so sharp to me is love—— that I fain in

vol-dray-e vo——ir, or scet bien de voir la belle a qui suis——
deep sea would drown—— me, for o, she knows well she whose slave I am——

que nul bien a-voir sans el-le ne—— puis.
that with-out her love no good can I—— have.

16. Gilles Binchois
Chanson, *Adieu m'amour et ma maistresse*

Together with the progressive, monumental style employed in the
composition of Masses, the Burgundians continued to cultivate in their
secular music the instrumentally accompanied chanson of the type established by Machaut. In these works there is less of the latter's harmonic
harshness, although many features of the *Ars nova* period are still present.
The Burgundian chansons are characterized by a texture that, though
polyphonic, does not exploit contrapuntal devices such as imitation. The
example given is by the leading master at the Dijon court, whose name
is usually associated with that of Dufay. The intimate, melancholy tone
of the text is common to many of these songs. Nearly all are in three
voices, the upper intended for a solo voice, perhaps doubled by an instrument, which in any case probably played the textless interludes. The
two lower parts (*tenor* and *contratenor*) were performed by instruments. It will be noted that the lower parts often cross in this composition, and that the contratenor begins and ends above the tenor. The two
lower voices differ in key signature from the *superius* (or *cantus*), an
example of "partial signature." The cadence formula employed throughout is still substantially that of the *Ars nova*, so far as the motion of the
upper voice is concerned.

Source: Oxford, Bodleian, Canonici Misc., 213, fol. 86.

16. Gilles Binchois (c. 1400–1460)

Chanson, *Adieu m'amour et ma maistresse*

[Note values halved]

[CT]

[T]

1.4.7. A - dieu m'a - mour et — ma mai - strais___se,___
Fare - well my love and — my dear la___dy,___
3. J'ay grant de - sir de — prendre a - dres___se,___
Long - ing shall help me — plan in se___cret,___
5. Sou - ven - gne vous, bel — le de - es___se,___
Do not for - get, O — love - ly god___dess,___

A - dieu mon sou - ve___
Fare - well my so - ve___
Pour - quoy vous pui - se___
How I may see you___
De moy qui sui vo,___
Your slave who serves you___

rain___ de___sir,
reign___ de___sire,
re___ve___ir,
yet___ a___gain,
sans___ fail___lir,
with___out___ fail,

2.8. A - dieu celle a___ qui___ veul___ ser___vir,___
Fare - well to her___ whom___ I___ would___ serve,___
6. En vo - lon - te___ de___ re___ve___nir,___
And in the thought___ of___ that___ re___turn,___

* C in MS.

A - dieu mon   con - fort
Fare - well   my   so - lace
Pen - sant a   vo bel -
Doth think up - on your

et   li - es_____se._____
and   my heart's_____ joy._____
le   jou - nes_____ se._____
love - ly   beau_____ty._____

17. Johannes Ockeghem
Sanctus (first section) from the "Missa prolationum"

Holy, holy, holy, Lord God of Hosts.

In the generation after Dufay the technical resources of polyphony were greatly expanded by Ockeghem and his school, who developed the technique of imitation into a style principle of transcendent importance. Their exploitation of canonic writing of the utmost skill and complexity, and their dexterity in using the devices of augmentation, diminution, inversion, and cancrizans have caused critics to place great emphasis upon this aspect of their music, somewhat to the neglect of its more expressive qualities. Ockeghem was the leader of the Flemish school in the generation after Binchois (who may have been Ockeghem's teacher),[1] and his art is usually represented as the epitome of late fifteenth-century contrapuntal ingenuity. Ockeghem's mastery of the imitative principle is strikingly demonstrated in the "Missa prolationum" (Prolation Mass), which may be described as a cycle of double canons (of which several are "augmentation canons") in which the successive sections begin with the unison, and progress, interval by interval, to the octave. Only two voices are supplied by the composer, the other two being derived from the notated pair, the proper interval at which they are to be sung being indicated by the position of the time signatures on the staves, or by the position of the clefs. In the opening section of the Sanctus given here, the soprano (*superius*) is a strict canon of the alto (*contratenor* in the original), entering at the distance of a sixth above in bar 13. Likewise the tenor, entering simultaneously with the soprano, is a strict canon of the bass, also at the sixth above. The fact that the highly ingenious construction of the work does not interfere with its musical expressiveness has caused its composer to be compared to Bach, and the "Missa Prolationum" has been aptly called "the *Art of Fugue* * of the fifteenth century," although an even more striking comparison could be made with Bach's *Goldberg Variations*. The original notation of this and other Masses by Ockeghem makes apparent his extraordinary rhythmic skill in a way that is not revealed by modern notation. For instance, the two upper voices are in what is known as the "major prolation" (triple measure), the two lower voices in the "minor prolation" (duple measure), as indicated by the original time signatures which appear at the beginning of the example.

Source: Rome, Biblioteca Vaticana, Chigiana, Cod. C. VIII, 234.
         Facsimile: Johannes Ockeghem, Collected Works, Vol. II (American Musicological Society, Studies and Documents, No. 1), New York, 1947, Plate VII.
         Transcription: *Ibid.*, p. 31.

* The "Art of Fugue" is described on p. 230.

17. Johannes Ockeghem (c. 1425–1495)
Sanctus (first section) from the "Missa prolationum"

[Note values halved]

18. Jacob Obrecht
Motet, *Parce, Domine*

Have mercy, O Lord, on Thy people,
For Thou art kind and merciful.
Hear us forever, O Lord.

This motet by Obrecht is another example of the extraordinary technical skill and expressiveness developed by Flemish composers during the last half of the fifteenth century. Obrecht and his teacher Ockeghem were the leading masters in this period of transition between the relatively archaic style of Dufay and the highly refined mastery of Josquin des Prez. The composers of this period greatly advanced the principles of canonic and imitative writing, of expressive harmony, and they articulated their music into clear phrases with appropriate cadence points. *Parce, Domine* shows the characteristic Flemish use of free contrapuntal lines with occasional suggestions of imitation. In this case the interplay of motives occurs only between the two upper voices; the melodic simplicity of the lowest voice is in great contrast. A feeling for the sense of the words is apparent, and the cadences make effective use of suspensions. This composition was used as an illustration of the Aeolian mode in the *Dodekachordon* of Glareanus, an important sixteenth-century theoretical work in which the traditional system of eight modes is extended to twelve. The musical illustrations in that book make it an important anthology of fifteenth-century masterpieces.

Source: Glareanus, *Dodekachordon*, Basle, 1547, p. 260.

18. Jacob Obrecht (c. 1430–1505)
Motet, *Parce, Domine*

19. Josquin des Prez
Motet, *Ave Maria*

Hail, Mary, full of grace, the Lord is with thee; blessed art thou among women, and blessed the fruit of thy womb, Jesus Christ, Son of the living God. And blessed be thy breasts, that have suckled the King of Kings and the Lord our God.

In the work of Josquin des Prez, the pupil of Ockeghem, and by far the greatest musical figure of the early sixteenth century, the development which began with the Burgundians comes to full fruition, and we enter the period of the High Renaissance. This motet represents a technique of composition much practiced by composers of Josquin's time, and equally by those of the next generation, in which a Gregorian melody is used as the source of the thematic material, but not reproduced literally. At times a phrase of the chant occurs in one part in longer notes than those prevailing in the other voices, as in the soprano, bars 11–13, but usually no one voice is thus distinguished from the others. The original material is treated very freely as to rhythm, and a good deal of ornamenting and filling-out of melodic leaps with added notes is applied to it.* In this piece the essentials of the mature sixteenth-century technique of motet composition are clearly present, in spite of differences of detail. Each phrase of the text is treated separately, usually in imitation, but at times in a homophonic style, or in a mixture of the two types. The beginning of a new phrase in one voice overlaps the end of the previous phrase in other voices, so that the texture is continuous. Important points of articulation are marked by full cadences, but the composer, by overlapping voices, insures that there shall be no break even at these points, unless for a special change of style, as at bar 42, where the section in

* The first part of the Solesmes version of this chant is shown at the end of the example.

triple time begins. Particularly characteristic of Josquin are the passages where the voices are presented in pairs, as in bars 20–23 and 43–46. The absence of the third from the final chord at the most important cadences should also be noted, and especially the manner in which, at the end of the composition, the alto voice, which at first has the third, abandons it. The persistence at this date of the so-called "Landini cadence" (bar 11) is also of interest.* (Since the two middle voices have substantially the same range, it is suggested that when the motet is sung by a mixed chorus these parts be performed by a combination of alto and tenor voices on each.)

Source: Berlin, Prussian State Library, Mus. m. 40013, fol. 170.
        Modern edition: Josquin des Prez, *Werke*, Motets, Vol. I, Amsterdam, 1935, p. 1.
Source of Gregorian chant: *Liber usualis* (Edition No. 801), Tournai, 1934, p. 1861.

* The "Landini cadence" is explained on p. 40.

19. Josquin des Prez (c. 1450–1521)
Motet, *Ave Maria*

The chant "Ave Maria"

[Original a perfect fourth lower]

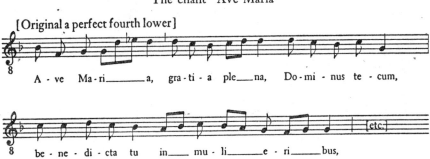

A - ve Ma - ri____a, gra - ti - a ple____na, Do - mi - nus te - cum,

be - ne - di - cta tu in____ mu - li____e - ri____bus, [etc.]

20. Thomas Crequillon
Chanson, *Pour ung plaisir*

21. Andrea Gabrieli
Canzona francese *deta Pour ung plaisir*

The French *chanson* occupies a position of great importance in the work of those composers of the early sixteenth century who represent the last phase of Netherlands domination, and was still more actively cultivated by French composers later in the century. The general structure of the chanson of this period was similar to that of the motet, but its rhythm and texture were simpler, as befitted the lightness of its text; its sections were shorter and more clearly defined, and unlike the motet and the more elaborate sixteenth-century madrigal it made extensive use of symmetrical repetitions of whole sections of music to different lines of text. Thus, in the present example by Crequillon, a Netherlander of considerable reputation with his contemporaries, the music of the first two lines of the poem (bars 1–13) is literally repeated for the following lines (bars 14–27), and in the last pair of lines both text and music are repeated. A characteristic of the opening of many chansons, a repeated-note figure in the rhythm ♩ ♩ ♩, is also a feature of the instrumental canzona which developed from the chanson.

Source: *Premier livre des chansons à quatre parties* . . . Tylman Susato, Antwerp, 1543.

The popularity of the French chanson in Italy resulted in frequent arrangements of these pieces for keyboard or lute, under the name *canzona francese*.* This process of arrangement was also applied to other types of vocal music, both sacred and secular. The method of instrumental transcription is illustrated by Example 21, a treatment by Andrea Gabrieli, the great Venetian master of the mid-sixteenth century, of Crequillon's chanson, Example 20. To facilitate comparison the keyboard version is here given directly beneath the original. The transcriber follows his model closely, but frequently divides the notes of one voice part or another into notes of shorter value that are arranged in pattern figurations, a procedure variously called "diminution," "coloration," or "division." This occurs most frequently toward the ends of sections, and on cadences. Such transcriptions as this soon led to the canzona francese as an independent instrumental form.**

Source: A. Gabrieli, *Canzoni alla francese et ricercari ariosi.* Libro quatro, Venice, 1605.

* The popularity of Crequillon's chanson is attested by keyboard versions by Cabezon (unpublished) and Bernhard Schmid the older (*Tabulaturbuch*, 1577), as well as by a ricercar on its themes by A. Gabrieli that occurs in the same publication as the present canzona.
** See p. 96.

20. Thomas Crequillon (d. c. 1557), Chanson, *Pour ung plaisir*

21. Andrea Gabrieli (c. 1510–1586), Canzona francese *deta*
Pour ung plaisir

22. Lute Dances
Der Prinzen-Tanz; Proportz

The lute played an important part in the rapid development of instrumental music that occurred in the latter part of the sixteenth century. During that period it occupied a position as a domestic instrument comparable with that of the piano today. Lute music was written in a special notation called *tablature*, which represented graphically, by means of lines and letters (or numerals), the position of the player's left hand on the finger board, and the strings to be plucked by the right. This method of notation was sometimes employed for keyboard music, the position of the fingers on the keyboard being indicated in a similar manner. The large number of manuscripts in lute tablature, as well as printed books, by composers in Italy, Spain, France, England, and Germany include dances, canzonas, *ricercars* and *fantasias*, pieces in improvisatory style, and "colored" (ornamented) transcriptions of vocal pieces both sacred and secular.* Dance movements greatly influenced the development of instrumental music in general because of their clear-cut, periodic structure, and their use of variation to avoid mere repetition. This example illustrates a principle widely practiced in the dance music of this period: that of following a slow dance in duple meter with a lively transformation of the first into triple meter. In Germany such a pair of dances was usually called *Tanz und Nachtanz* ("dance and after-dance"); here the name "Proportz" applied to the Nachtanz refers to its being a rhythmic transformation of the Tanz. In the late sixteenth century the commonest pair of dances, for keyboard and ensemble as well as for lute, was the

* Examples of certain of these forms may be found on pages 66, 98, and 145.

pavane and *galliard*. In the seventeenth century the association of several dances led to the *suite*.*

Source: MS addition to a copy of R. Wyssenbach, *Tabulaturbuch uff die Lutten*, Zürich, 1550.
Transcription: W. Tappert, *Sang und Klang aus alter Zeit*, Berlin, 1906, p. 54.

* See p. 147.

22. Lute Dances (c. 1550)

Der Prinzen-Tanz; Proportz

23. Orlandus Lassus
Motet, *Tristis est anima mea*

RESPOND FOR MAUNDY THURSDAY

My soul is exceeding sorrowful, even unto death: tarry ye here, and watch with me: now ye will see the multitude that will surround me: ye will take flight, and I shall go to be sacrificed for you.

Orlandus Lassus, born in the Netherlands, became in the course of an active life a world figure, and contributed to every type of vocal music practiced in the later sixteenth century, writing not only Masses and motets, but secular compositions to Italian, French, and German texts. This motet (and Example 25 as well) exhibits the final development of the form as it was brought to perfection at the end of the century. Each phrase of the text is accorded the most imaginative treatment in order to bring out the thought embodied in the words. The rhythms of the individual voices are very free and independent of one another, following the natural accentuation of the words. The accents of the separate voices frequently are at variance with each other, but their independent rhythms are superimposed in such a way that the effect of a rather regular duple meter in the ensemble is produced, a feature of most sacred choral music of this period. Lassus employs here the five-part medium most frequently used in the later sixteenth century, but makes a special point of a top voice widely separated in range from the others, to produce at the outset (bars 5–6 and 9–10) a vivid emotional interpretation of the word "tristis." Another instance of expressive interpretation of the text is seen in his employment at the word "mortem" in bar 14 of a final chord without the third, by this date a rather unusual occurrence, but

here used deliberately. Again, he gives a special impressiveness to the
text in bars 28–35 and 49–59 by a change to chordal style, and in bars
37–40 the successive entries of the voices on a theme beginning with a
short note convey the excitement of the phrase "quae circumdabit me."
Such musical illustration of the text is not uncommon in this style, though
it is more frequently found in secular than in sacred music.

Source: O. Lassus, *Magnum Opus Musicum*, No. 172 (a collection of all the
motets of Lassus, published posthumously in 1604 by his sons).
Modern edition: Orlando di Lasso, *Sämtliche Werke*, Vol. V, Leipzig, 1895, p. 48.

23. Orlandus Lassus (1532–1594)
Motet, *Tristis est anima mea*

[Note values halved]

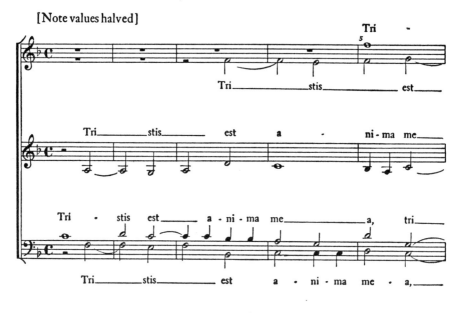

24. Giovanni Pierluigi da Palestrina
Agnus Dei (I) from the Mass "Veni sponsa Christi"

O Lamb of God, that takest away the sins of the world,
    have mercy upon us.
Antiphon: Come, Bride of Christ, accept the crown
    which the Lord has prepared for thee in all eternity.

Unlike most composers of the sixteenth century, Palestrina devoted himself almost exclusively to church music, and his name has become a sort of symbol for the highly refined polyphonic art of the late Renaissance. Palestrina's Mass "Veni sponsa Christi" belongs to the class called *Parody Mass:* that is, it is modeled upon a pre-existing work, in this case a motet by Palestrina himself.* It was a common practice in the fifteenth and sixteenth centuries to use not only one's own compositions for this purpose, but those of others, and to use secular as well as sacred pieces. In this particular instance the question of the source of the material is further complicated by the fact that the motet used as a basis for the Mass is itself written on the Gregorian antiphon on this text.** The chant themes can readily be traced in the section of the Mass here given: "Agnus Dei" uses the theme of "Veni sponsa Christi"; "qui tollis" that of "accipe coronam"; "miserere" that of "quam tibi Dominus." But this

* It should be noted that the word "parody" in this connection has the sense of "borrowing" and conveys nothing of the usual connotation of "ridiculing."
** See the Gregorian antiphon melody given at the end of the example. The first version here given is that of the Solesmes edition, which is now approved by the Church as the authentic form. The second is that of the so-called "Editio Medicea," a version of the chant published soon after the death of Palestrina, and with whose editing he was once reputed to have been connected. A comparison of the theme in the Mass at the words "qui tollis" with the "Medicea" version of the phrase "accipe coronam" shows that the latter represents the form of the chant used by Palestrina in writing his motet.

does not mean that the Mass is based upon this material directly, though such a method was often used at this time. For the motet itself clearly reappears in the Mass; for instance, in the *Kyrie* Palestrina reproduces substantially his whole motet, the correspondence being perfectly exact in all the parts for many bars at a time. As the Mass proceeds the treatment of the motet material becomes more and more diversified, a technique not unlike that used in a set of variations.* As this example shows, the same principles of construction used in the motet of this time are employed in the Mass. The perfect smoothness of contrapuntal technique here shown, the flowing lines, the open texture, the delicate handling of dissonances and the rather cool atmosphere of the whole are highly characteristic of Palestrina.

Source: Ioannis Petraloysii Praenestini, *Missarum—Liber Nonus*, Venice, 1599.
Modern edition: Ioannis Petraloysii Praenestini, *Opera omnia*, Vol. 18, Leipzig, 1886, p. 35.
Source of Antiphon:
    1) *Liber usualis* (Edition No. 801), Tournai, 1934, p. 1214.
    2) *Compendium antiphonarii et breviarii Romani*, Ratisbon, 1888, p. [43].

* The four sections of the motet, which correspond to the four phrases of the original chant text, reappear in the Mass at the following points, among others:
Veni—at "Kyrie," "et in terra," "qui tollis," "et expecto," "sanctus," "Benedictus," "Agnus" (I and II).
accipe—at "Christe," "et in Terra," "Domine Deus," "Hosanna," "Qui Tollis."
quam tibi—at "Kyrie" II, "Cum sancto," "Patrem," "pleni," "in nomine."
praeparavit—at "Kyrie" II, "propter magnam," "et vitam venturi," "gloria tua," "dona."

24. Giovanni Pierluigi da Palestrina (c. 1525–1594)
Agnus Dei (I) from the Mass "Veni sponsa Christi"

[Original a major 2nd higher. Note values halved]

Antiphon: *Veni sponsa Christi*

25. William Byrd
Motet, *Ego sum panis vivus*

I am the living bread which came down from heaven:
if any man eat of this bread, he shall live forever.
Alleluia. St. John 6:51.

In the music of William Byrd, the contemporary of Palestrina and
Lassus, and perhaps the greatest composer that England has produced,
the native English gifts of melodic freshness and vigorous rhythm find
full expression. In this motet, whose formal organization perfectly ex-
emplifies the principles described in the notes on page 58, the melodic
lines are much more angular and distinctive than in many Continental
sacred compositions of the period. The rhythms of the individual parts
are so free and powerful that they even modify the rhythm of the ensemble, so that it is necessary to employ bars of irregular lengths in an
edition in modern notation. (The value of the quarter note remains constant throughout.) An extensive use of "tone-painting" is seen in this work,
and this is often applied to the setting of individual words with great literal-
ness: thus, "coelo" (heaven) is invariably set to the highest note of the
phrase in which it occurs, and "descendi" (descended) is set to a falling
figure. In a less literal manner, the lively triple rhythms at "vivet in
aeternum" express the joy of the believer at the expectation of eternal
life. In the "Alleluia" section, whose high spirits and brilliance are very
characteristic of Byrd, the extended use of harmonic and melodic sequences, first falling, then rising, is a feature not commonly found in the
work of Palestrina and Lassus. The cross-relation in bar 28 between tenor
and soprano is a detail often found in the music of English composers at
this time. It is a deliberately calculated point of style, not a crudity.

Source: W. Byrd, *Gradualia*, Liber secundus, London, 1607.
Modern edition: *Tudor Church Music*, Vol. 7, London, 1927, p. 251.

25. William Byrd

Motet, *Ego sum panis vivus*

[Original a minor 3rd lower. Note values halved]

Note: The value of the quarter note remains constant in bars of varying lengths.

qui de coe - lo de - scen_____ di.

de - scen_____ di, de - scen_____ di.

lo de - scen - di, de coe_____ lo de - scen_____

scen_____ di, de - scen_____ di. Si

Si quis man - du - ca - ve -

Si quis man - du - ca - ve - rit,

di. Man - du - ca_____ ve - rit, si

quis man - du - ca - ve - rit, si

rit, si quis man - du - ca - ve - rit ex hoc pa_____

si quis man - du - ca - ve - rit ex hoc pa_____

quis man - du - ca - ve - rit ex hoc pa_____

quis man - du - ca - ve - rit ex hoc pa_____

_____ne, vi_____vet in ae - ter -

_____ne, vi_____vet in ae - ter_____

_____ne, vi - vet in_____ ae - ter -

_____ne,

26. Keyboard Canzona
Canzona per l'epistola

The popular vocal chanson continued to exert its influence in the field of late Renaissance and early Baroque instrumental music. In keyboard composition it was the source of numerous *canzoni alla francese*, such as the example by A. Gabrieli (page 66), that were mere transcriptions with instrumental coloration added. A step in the direction of more independent character and a more instrumental conception is seen in the anonymous *Canzona per l'epistola*. Certain features common to most vocal chansons remain: the characteristic repeated-note opening motive, the clear sectional divisions, and the general clarity and liveliness of style. The whole effect of this canzona, though, is that of an instrumentally contrived piece, with its wide range of voices (as compared with the Gabrieli example), its angular second subject, its general gait, and its toccata-like ending. In the further history of the canzona the form as used in the instrumental ensemble (*canzona da sonare*) became more extended, alternating contrapuntal and homophonic sections, and finally became identified with the *sonata da chiesa* (page 162). The keyboard canzona (*canzona d'organo*), on the other hand, became more concentrated in form, as in those of Frescobaldi where the subject of each section was a varied form of the initial motive, so that the canzona, like the monothematic ricercar, was an important precursor of the fugue. The significance of the title of this example lies in the fact that it was written as a substitute for the choir in part of the liturgy of the Mass, like Example 34 (page 145).

In this case it followed the Epistle, taking the place of the Gradual and Alleluia.

Source: A manuscript collection of early seventeenth-century keyboard music in the possession of Laurence K. J. Feininger. According to Dr. Alfred Einstein, most of the compositions in this manuscript seem to be by Ercole Pasquini (b. c. 1580), the predecessor of Frescobaldi as organist of St. Peter's in Rome.

Note: The notation of the cadential figures in such places as bars 27, 30, 40, and 53, and of the final flourish of bars 51 and 52, has been preserved as it appears in the original manuscript. Although these passages would be somewhat differently written in the more precise notation of our time, the intention of the composer seems clear enough.

26. Keyboard Canzona (early 17th c.)

Canzona per l'epistola

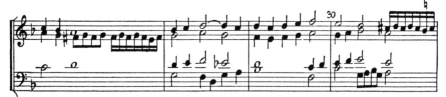

27. Luca Marenzio
Madrigal, *S'io parto, i' moro*

The brilliant life of the wealthy and pleasure-loving courts of Renaissance Italy fostered a lively cultivation of the arts, and their active enjoyment and appreciation by cultured men and women. This was strikingly manifested in the large amount of secular vocal music produced, most of it intended for performance by amateur music-lovers for their own pleasure. In Italy the most important of a number of forms composed for this purpose was the madrigal (not connected with the *Ars nova* composition of the same name). Musically the madrigal was similar to the motet of the same period in its treatment of the text phrase by phrase in separate sections, but the tone and style were much lighter, as befitted the secular character of the poems set, of which love was most often the subject. Marenzio, who lived in the second half of the sixteenth century, is generally considered the greatest Italian madrigalist, a reputation that he enjoyed even in his own lifetime. His work is sensitive and poetic, often in a quite serious vein, in contrast to the lightness most often associated with the madrigal style. The treatment of the text is always highly expressive of the mood of the poem, but Marenzio avoids the more obvious and literal uses of musical illustration, contenting himself with subtle touches like the expressive rest in bar 4 of the soprano part, which gives an effect of a voice choked by emotion, or the rising tension in the second tenor in bars 45–47. He makes less consistent use of imitation than do many Italian and English madrigalists. This preference for a more harmonic style, and in general an interest in the direct expression of emotion, presages the change that was coming over all vocal music toward the end of his career. In England the importation of books of Italian madrigals gave rise, in the latter part of the sixteenth century, to an outpouring of works in the same style which produced a distinctively English school of madrigal composition (illustrated on page 110).

Source: L. Marenzio, *Il sesto libro de madrigali a cinque voci*, Venice, 1594. Modern edition: Luca Marenzio, *Sämtliche Werke*, Vol. 2; *Publikationen älterer Musik*, Jahrg. 6, Leipzig, 1931, p. 103.

27. Luca Marenzio (c. 1560–1599)
Madrigal, *S'io parto, i' moro*

Note: The value of the quarter note remains constant in bars of varying lengths.

28. John Bennet
Madrigal, *Thyrsis, Sleepest Thou?*

The English interest in madrigal composition, which was given its first impetus by the importation of books of Italian madrigals, and the publication of Italian works translated into English (notably *Musica transalpina*, 1588), gave rise before the close of the sixteenth century to a flourishing English school of composition. By the first quarter of the seventeenth century this group of composers had published hundreds of works in this form, many of them as fine as their Italian models. John Bennet, who lived in the later sixteenth and early seventeenth centuries, and who is represented in the famous madrigal collection, *The Triumphs of Oriana* (1601), is not as profound a composer as the greatest Englishmen working in this field, such as Weelkes and Wilbye, but his technical mastery of the lighter sort of madrigal was second to none. This characteristic example is set to a pastoral text in the true Renaissance tradition. In the music which clothes this text, the type of tone-painting known as "madrigalism" is vividly illustrated by such touches as the graphic setting of "sleepest thou?" with its lively overlapping triple rhythms, and the naïve but charming illustration, perfectly executed, of individual words such as "cuckoo," and "sighed." The great variety of texture, with quick alternations of chordal writing and imitative treatment, is also typical. The freshness of melodic invention, and still more the springlike atmosphere of the whole composition, characterize a great many of the Elizabethan madrigals. The *ballet*, or *fa la*, in which a chordal texture and dancelike rhythm predominate, and in which a refrain to the syllables "fa la" is a special feature, was actually much less important than the type shown here. Only three English composers, Morley, Weelkes, and Tomkins, wrote ballets, while the pastoral madrigal was practiced by all English madrigal composers.

Source: John Bennet, *Madrigals to Four Voices*, London, 1599, No. 8.

28. John Bennet (c. 1575–c. 1625)
Madrigal, *Thyrsis, Sleepest Thou?*

[Original a major 2nd higher]

*In performance it is suggested that Tenor and Bass exchange parts in the passage between * bar 12 and * bar 17.

Note: The value of the quarter note remains constant in bars of varying lengths.

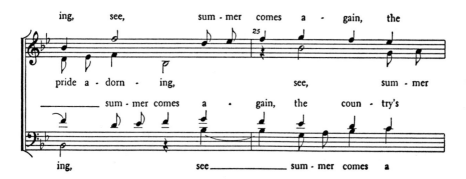

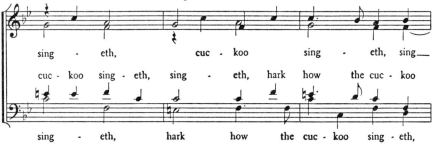

29. Giles Farnaby
Variations for Virginals, *Loth to Depart*

A perfected style of idiomatic keyboard music first appears in English compositions for the type of harpsichord known as the virginals, during the late sixteenth and early seventeenth centuries. The keyboard style of such composers as Byrd, Philips, Farnaby, Bull, Tomkins, and Gibbons was derived entirely from the nature of the instrument and evidences a high order of virtuosity. The virginalist literature comprises dances such as the pavane and galliard, variations, preludes in improvisatory style, the polyphonic fantasia or "fancy" (English names for the *ricercar*), a special *cantus firmus* type called the *In Nomine*, and transcriptions of vocal pieces. The highest achievements of the virginalists were embodied in sets of variations, which were usually on folk melodies or popular songs. This piece is characteristic of the style of many contemporary sets, with its brief passages of both strict and free imitation, its fluent figuration and ornamental cadences, its many "false relations," and its occasional complexity of rhythmic texture. Farnaby, whose brief life appears to have passed within the second half of the sixteenth century, is represented by over fifty compositions in the great *Fitzwilliam Virginal Book*, a collection of 297 pieces by nearly all the virginalists. Like many of the other virginalist composers, Farnaby was also active as a composer of madrigals. The manner of executing the ornaments indicated by the signs at bars 7, 13, and 35 in this example is uncertain. The irregular barring of the original manuscript is here preserved.

Source: *Fitzwilliam Virginal Book* (Fitzwilliam Museum, Cambridge).
Modern edition: *Fitzwilliam Virginal Book*, Vol. II, London, 1899, p. 317.

29. Giles Farnaby (c. 1560–c. 1600)
Variations for Virginals, *Loth to Depart*

30. Giulio Caccini
Madrigal for Solo Voice and Lute
Dovrò dunque morire

The publication of Caccini's *Le Nuove musiche* (*New Music*) in 1602 provided a convenient name for a revolutionary change in the fundamental approach of composers to the problems of vocal and instrumental music which took place about the beginning of the seventeenth century. The period thus inaugurated, known as the Baroque, brought forth the new vocal forms of opera, oratorio, and cantata, and the instrumental innovations of concerto, sonata, suite, and fugue. Caccini, who wrote the first opera to be presented in a public theater (1600), claimed to be the originator of a new vocal solo style, termed the *stile rappresentativo*. The expressed purpose of the new vocal music was to do away with every device which might interfere with the most direct expression of the sentiment of the text. Polyphonic texture and contrapuntal development were discarded in favor of *accompanied monody*, in which a single expressive vocal line was projected upon a harmonic background. The accompanist, using a keyboard instrument or lute, improvised this background above a single line of bass notes, guided by figures above or below the notes (hence "figured bass"), and by certain conventions which soon became established. This device, called variously *basso continuo*, *Generalbass*, or *thorough-bass*, by reason of its constant presence throughout the composition, soon became an indispensable foundation for all Baroque ensemble music, instrumental as well as vocal. Caccini's own published version of the present example consisted only of the voice line and the bass with its sparse figuring. The "realization" here given of the harmonies indicated or implied is that of Robert Dowland, an Eng-

lish lutenist, who published a version of this composition with the accompanying filling-out in tablature * in 1610. In accordance with the
practice of lutenist composers at this period, Dowland's realization is
definitely contrapuntal. He does not follow Caccini's figuring in certain
small details, and introduces a few variants into the voice part which are
here adopted. The angularity of the melody, and the directness of utter-
ance, are in striking contrast to the musical tradition of the period just
preceding 1600, and the emotional use of coloratura at the final cadence
is another sign pointing to a new era. It should be noted that Caccini,
contrary to later practice, indicates the precise octave of the note he
wishes used in the filling-out.

Sources: *Le Nuove musiche di Giulio Caccini, detto Romano*, Florence, 1602.
    (Facsimile edition published by Reale Accademica d'Italia, 1934.)
    R. Dowland, *A Musical Banquet*, London, 1610.

* For a description of lute tablature see p. 74.

30. Giulio Caccini (c.1560–1618)
Madrigal for Solo Voice and Lute,
Dovrò dunque morire

ta, Non____ po-ter dir a voi "Mo____ro, mia
pled, Ne____ver to say to thee, "O____ now I

vi - ta." O____ mi - se - ria in-au-di____
pe - rish." O____ what grief un-ex-am____

ta, Non po-ter dir a voi "Mo - ro, mia vi -
pled, Ne-ver to say to thee, "Fare-well, be - lo -

ta." Non____ po-ter dir a voi "Mo____ro, mia
ved." Ne____ver to say to thee, "Fare____well, be -

vi - ta mo____ro,____ mia____ vi____ta."
lo - ved, fare____well,____ be____lo____ved."

• Nuove Musiche:

31. Claudio Monteverdi
Recitative from "Orfeo," *Tu se' morta*

The most important direct result of experiments with the new accompanied monody in Florence in the late sixteenth century was the creation of opera. The earliest composers to attempt the new form, preoccupied with the exact rendering of the natural accents of the text, invented as a vehicle for this purpose a type of free declamation almost completely devoid of purely melodic development, which simply followed the details of the text from one emotional point to the next. This wandering, declamatory music, soon known as *recitative*, was supported by the continuo only. The lyrical element, which later developed into the *aria*, was almost completely absent from the earliest operas.* The chorus played a very small part, and the whole orchestra was rarely used except for introductions and interludes between scenes. A tremendous advance in the whole apparatus of the opera was made by Monteverdi, who lived until nearly the middle of the seventeenth century, and was the first opera composer of genius. Unlike Peri and Caccini, he used the orchestra for dramatic effects. In the printed score of Monteverdi's "Orfeo," indications of the participation of various instruments, mostly of the continuo variety, are occasionally given. In this scene, where Orpheus, having learned of Euridice's death, expresses his determination to abandon the earth and follow her to the lower regions, the instruments prescribed are a small portable organ and a bass lute, both of which presumably realized the harmonies from the figured bass. The realization here given is more literal than that of many modern editors, and, it is hoped, will convey more accurately the effect of Monteverdi's intensely dramatic use of dissonance for emotional expressiveness. The version has been so con-

* Concerning the later recitative and aria see p. 189.

trived that by omitting the notes of the voice part itself (here given an octave higher than the tenor range prescribed by the composer) it will serve to accompany a singer. The barring of the original edition, which is wholly without rhythmic significance, has been altered to make the subtleties of Monteverdi's declamation more readily apparent.

Source: *L'Orfeo, Favola in Musica,* da Claudio Monteverdi, Venice, 1609 (Facsimile edition, Augsburg, 1927).

31. Claudio Monteverdi (1567–1643)
Recitative from "Orfeo," *Tu se' morta*

Note: The value of the quarter note remains constant in bars of varying lengths.

32. Giacomo Carissimi
Scene from "Judicium Salomonis," *Afferte gladium*

Oratorio, like opera, appeared at the very beginning of the seventeenth century, and was at first distinguished from opera only by having a sacred libretto. Toward the middle of the century it definitely discarded the stage trappings of opera and took on the characteristics which established it as a distinct musical form of its own. The principal figure in this development was Carissimi, a Roman church musician of the seventeenth century. The work from which the present excerpt is taken begins with an instrumental introduction, after which the people are summoned together by the *historicus*, or narrator, a character common in sacred representations from the twelfth to the eighteenth centuries. Then follows the scene between Solomon and the two mothers, which is given in the example, after which a long, motet-like chorus praising the King's wisdom closes the work. The example illustrates the use of dramatic monody in presenting the Biblical story (I Kings 3:16–18). The original score has only two lines of music, those of the recitative and the bass, which is unfigured, and has been "realized" here for performance. The unfigured continuo is not uncommon in the Baroque period; the keyboard performers of the time were expected to be able to supply the needed harmonies even without the aid of figures. The "Judgment of Solomon" represents the shorter form of oratorio sometimes called the *cantata da chiesa* (church cantata), as distinguished from the full-length oratorio. A secular form of similar limited scope, which however almost never employs the chorus, was called the *cantata da camera* (chamber cantata).

Source: Carissimi, *Werke*, ed. by Fr. Chrysander, in: *Denkmäler der Tonkunst*, Vol. II, Hamburg, 1869. This volume also contains Carissimi's *Jephte, Baltazar,* and *Jonas*.

32. Giacomo Carissimi (1605–1674)
Scene from "Judicium Salomonis," *Afferte gladium*

[Original a major 2nd higher]

Solomon

Af - fer - te, af - fer - te gla - di - um et di - vi - di - te in - fan - tem
Go take thou the sword and se - ver the child, the liv - ing child in two, di -

vi - vum in du - as par - tes et da - te di - mi - di - am par - tem
vide thou the liv - ing in - fant, and give thou a half to the one and

u - ni et di - mi - di - am par - tem al - te - ri.
like - wise to the oth - er, give half the child to each.

2nd Mother

Rec - tum ju - di - ci - um tu - um, o rex. Nec
Right - eous and wise is thy judg - ment, O king. So

mi - hi nec ti - bi, nec mi - hi nec ti - bi; di___vi___
let it be nei - ther for one nor the o - ther, but___ di___

da - tur, di___vi___da___tur. Heu, heu,___ fi - li mi!
vide it, but___ di___vide___ it. Ah, ah,___ ah my son!

1st Mother

Com-mo - ta sunt vi - sce - ra me - a su - per te, fi - li
My heart doth yearn for thee. Yea, my heart doth yearn for thee, o my

mi! Da - te, da - te il - li po - ti - us in - fan - tem
son! Give to her the liv - ing child, to her the liv - ing

Solomon

vi - vum et non di - vi - da - tur.   Di - vi - di - te, di -
in - fant, and in no wise harm it.   Di - vide the child, di -

vi - di - te in - fan - tem, di - vi - di - te, di - vi - di - te in -
vide the child in two parts, di - vide the child, di - vide the child, the

2nd Mother

fan_____tem vi - vum.   Nec mi - hi nec ti - bi, nec mi - hi nec
liv_____ing in - fant.   So let it be nei - ther for one nor the

ti - bi; di____vi____da - tur, di____vi____da_____tur.
o - ther, but__ di__vide it; yea,__ di____vide_____it .

1st Mother

Heu,   heu,   non,   non di - vi - da - tur!   Da - te
Ah,   ah,   no,   do not di - vide it!   Give to

da - te il - li po - ti - us in - fan - tem
her the liv - ing child, to her the liv - ing

vi - vum et non di - vi - da - tur.
in - fant, and in no wise harm it.

Solomon

Da - te hu - ic in - fan - tem vi - vum, da - te hu - ic in - fan - tem
Give to this one the liv - ing in - fant, give to this one the liv - ing

vi - vum: haec est en - im   ma - ter   e_____jus!
in - fant,   for she is   in - deed the   mo_____ther!

Da - te hu - ic in - fan - tem vi - vum, da - te hu - ic in - fan - tem
Give to this one the liv - ing in - fant, give to this one the liv - ing

vi - vum: haec est en - im ma - ter   e - jus, haec est en - im ma - ter
in - fant,   for she is in - deed the   mo - ther, for she is in - deed the

e_____jus!
mo_____ther!

33. Heinrich Schütz
Sacred Cantata (Concerto), *O Herr, hilf*

Along with the Florentine experiments with accompanied monody, which led to opera, composers associated with the great cathedral of St. Mark's in Venice occupied themselves with the problems of combining voices and instruments, often composing on a grand scale for several complete choruses, a style known as *polychoric*. The German Heinrich Schütz, who was born one hundred years before J. S. Bach, became a pupil of the last and greatest of these Venetian masters, Giovanni Gabrieli, and brought the new style back to Germany, founding a school of composition in which the monodic style and the combination of choirs of voices and instruments began a development of Protestant church music that culminated in the work of J. S. Bach a century later. This example is called a *concerto* by the composer. The term in this instance means little more than an ensemble (concerted) piece for voices and instruments, a meaning the word still retained, along with new implications, in the early eighteenth century. This example shows the beginnings of an idiomatic instrumental style in the treatment of the violins, but there is an equally obvious tendency to treat the violins and voices as interchangeable (see bar 67 ff), thus foreshadowing the typical Baroque "instrumental" style of writing for voices. Equally significant in the new style is the combination of a contrapuntal texture with the specifically harmonic background furnished by the continuo. A further important element in the formation of the Baroque style is the strong rhythmic organization that Schütz and his contemporaries brought to the new music, in contrast to the almost complete lack of definite metrical organization in the earliest accompanied monody. An important detail of style is the treatment of the rhythm at cadence points in the section in triple time (see bars 38–39, 42–43, 46–47,

56–57, 59–60) where the accents of two bars of three-four time are re-arranged in such a way that a single bar of three-two time results. This treatment of triple-time cadences is common throughout the entire Baroque period.* The use of extended melodic and harmonic sequences, especially in the final section, illustrates one of the most important developmental procedures of the Baroque period.

Source: Heinrich Schütz, *Symphoniarum sacrarum tertia pars*, Dresden, 1650. Modern edition: Heinrich Schütz, *Sämtliche Werke*, Vol. 10, Leipzig, 1891, pp. 54–57.

* This rhythmic effect, sometimes called *hemiola*, may also be seen in Example 36 (bars 16, 21, 26), and in Example 39, adagio movement (bars 8–9, 17–18, 22–23, 31–32, 36–37).

33. Heinrich Schütz (1585–1672)
Sacred Cantata (Concerto), *O Herr, hilf*

der   da   kömmt, der   da   kömmt   im   Na - men
he   that   comes, he   that   comes,   that   comes   in

kömmt,   der   da   kömmt   im   Na - men
comes,   he   that   comes,   that   comes   in

der   da   kömmt, der   da   kömmt   im   Na - men
he   that   comes, he   that   comes,   that   comes   in

des   Her - ren,   im   Na - men   des   Her -
the   Lord's   Name,   that   comes   in   the   Lord's

des   Her - ren,   im   Na - men   des   Her -
the   Lord's   Name,   that   comes   in   the   Lord's

des   Her - ren,   im   Na - men   des   Her -
the   Lord's   Name,   that   comes   in   the   Lord's

ren.   Ho - si - an___
Name.   Ho - si - an___

ren.   Ho - si -
Name.   Ho - si -

ren.   Ho - si - an - na   in   der   Hö - he.
Name.   Ho - si - an - na   in   the   high - est.

34. Girolamo Frescobaldi
Ricercar dopo il Credo, for Organ

The *ricercar*, sometimes called the *fantasia*, was an instrumental composition whose formal construction was similar to that of the sixteenth-century motet, with its successive subjects, each treated in the manner of a fugal exposition. The first ricercars appeared about the beginning of the sixteenth century, and were literal transcriptions for keyboard or lute of vocal motets, but by the middle of the century original compositions appear in growing numbers. Later, a more specifically instrumental character was taken on by the ricercar, and in the seventeenth century the number of subjects was reduced to one, a development that led directly to the fugue.* The present example by Frescobaldi, who was famous as an organist at St. Peter's in Rome during the first half of the seventeenth century, illustrates a point in the development of the ricercar that is very close to the fugue, in that a single subject supplies nearly all the important material of the piece. From bar 24 on, the subject appears in augmentation, with the exception of the final entry. The subject itself has the chromatic character that is a feature of many of Frescobaldi's themes. The *Fiori musicali* (*Musical Flowers*) in which this composition first appeared is a collection of organ pieces mainly intended for use in the celebration of the Mass, the present example coming after the Credo, as its title indicates.

Source: G. Frescobaldi, *Fiori musicali*, Venice, 1635. (An interesting preface by the composer himself occurs in this volume.)
Modern edition: Frescobaldi, *Collectio musices organicae*, edited by Franz Haberl, Leipzig, 1889, p. 36. This composition may also be found in a more recent edition of the *Fiori musicali* by Fernando Germani, Rome, 1936, p. 62.

* An example of the fugue occurs on p. 232.

34. Girolamo Frescobaldi (1583–1643)
Ricercar dopo il Credo, for Organ

[Note values halved]

35. Johann Jakob Froberger
Suite in E Minor, for Clavichord

Examples 11 and 22 (p. 34 and p. 76), together with this one, represent successive stages in the evolution of the dance suite, which became one of the most important forms of keyboard music during the Baroque period, maintaining its significance until the advent of the classical sonata. By Froberger's time the suite, while it kept the external rhythmic character of its dances, had already become stylized; it was more a series of intimate mood-pictures than a set of actual dances. The sequence of *allemande, courante, sarabande* and *gigue,* which came to be universally adopted, is attributed to Froberger, who traveled widely throughout Europe as a keyboard virtuoso during the second quarter of the seventeenth century. In Paris he came under the influence of the great French lutenists and the lute-inspired clavecinists. Features of lute style may be seen in the texture of this suite, particularly in the free appearance and disappearance of voices, the arbitrary doubling of parts in important chords, the arpeggiated cadences, and the use of ornaments.* Traces of these mannerisms remained in the suite even during the final period of its existence. After Froberger, other dance movements were often added between the sarabande and gigue, and a prelude sometimes placed at the beginning. In the suites of the late Baroque, especially those of J. S. Bach, each of the movements, though still retaining the characteristic binary form with repeats, became considerably longer, and more elaborate in texture.

Source: Vienna, State Library, MS 16798.
        Modern edition: DTOe, Vol. VI, Vienna, 1899, p. 64.

* In all Baroque music, trills begin with the upper (auxiliary) note, not with the main note.

35. Johann Jakob Froberger (1616–1667)
Suite in E Minor, for Clavichord

ALLEMANDE

COURANTE

SARABANDE

GIGUE

36. Jean Baptiste Lully
Overture to "Armide"

The operatic *overture* of the seventeenth century was of the greatest importance for the subsequent development of orchestral style and form. Throughout the Baroque period the type most generally employed was the *French overture*, which consisted of a broad, massive opening section, followed by a fugal allegro, and sometimes ending with another slow section similar to the opening, or, rarely, with a dance movement such as the minuet. The antecedents of the form have been traced back to the brief instrumental piece at the end of the first act of Cavalieri's "Rappresentazione di anima e di corpo" (1600). Cavalli, the most important of the opera composers who immediately succeeded Monteverdi, used an overture that foreshadowed the fully mature type, but the characteristic fugal style of the second section first appears in Luigi Rossi's "Erminia sul Giordano" (1627). The name of Lully, who was the operatic dictator of France during the later seventeenth century, is particularly associated with the French overture, which he used in all his operas, from "Thésée" (1673) to "Armide" (1685). The overture to the latter, which forms the present example, begins with a slow, stately introduction that employs the characteristic dotted rhythms seen in nearly all French overtures. The quick second section begins in a freely fugal manner, after which such imitation as appears is mostly confined to the outer parts, with the initial motive of the section sometimes appearing in inversion. The final section returns to the stately pace of the opening, to which it bears a strong resemblance. After Lully the French overture culminated in the work of Purcell, Bach, and Handel. As used by these later masters, the dotted effect of the rhythm of the opening section is greatly emphasized, and the fast section becomes very definitely fugal.

In the late Baroque the French overture was used not only to open dramatic works and oratorios, but also employed as a self-sufficient instrumental form, either alone or as the first movement of both orchestral and keyboard suites. Another type of overture practiced in the early eighteenth century was the *Italian overture* (often called *sinfonia*), whose distinctive features were an opening allegro, not in fugal style, followed by a lyrical slow section, and concluding with a lively, dancelike finale. Though less frequently employed in the Baroque period than the French overture, the Italian overture was of great importance for later periods, since it was one of the most important predecessors of the classical symphony.

Source: Lully, *Armide, tragédie mise en musique*, Paris, 1686.
A modern edition of the complete opera may be found in *Publikationen älterer praktischer und theoretischer Musikwerke* (R. Eitner, ed.), Bd. XIV, Leipzig, 1885, p. 1.

36. Jean Baptiste Lully (1632–1687)
Overture to "Armide"

37. Johann Pachelbel
Toccata in E Minor, for Organ

The most idiomatic keyboard style practiced in the Baroque period was that of the *toccata*. This term, derived from the Italian *toccare* (to touch), with its implication of free improvisation, applies to a style of writing, rather than a form. Most often composed for organ, the toccata is a piece which emphasizes extended virtuoso passages of a rhapsodic sort from which the regular rhythmic pulse, so salient a feature of most Baroque music, is almost wholly absent. The present example by Pachelbel, one of the important late seventeenth-century precursors of Bach in organ composition, exhibits many characteristic features. After a rhapsodic opening, and a passage employing striking dissonances, the composition settles down to the working out of a figure in sequences over a slow-moving bass. In the great toccatas of Bach these stylistic features are greatly developed, and extended sections in strict rhythm, often fugal in style, alternate with the rhapsodic passages. This composition was originally notated in tablature,* which was frequently employed by German composers for the organ, even as late as the time of Bach. The term *fantasia* is often used by Bach to designate a work in toccata style; in the sixteenth and seventeenth centuries *fantasia* was used as a title for compositions in the style of the ricercar (see Example 34, page 145).

Source: F. Commer, *Sammlung der besten Meisterwerke des 17. und 18. Jahrhunderts für die Orgel*, Berlin—Posen, n.d. (18—), p. 150.

* For a description of tablature see p. 74.

37. Johann Pachelbel (1653–1706)
Toccata in E Minor, for Organ

38. Henry Purcell
Ground for Harpsichord, *A New Ground*

The term *ground* identifies a composition written on a ground bass; that is, a melodic phrase of a few bars (usually four) which is repeated over and over to form the bass line of a composition whose upper parts are altered with the successive repetitions. The ground bass (*basso ostinato,* "obstinate bass") was an important structural device in seventeenth-century composition, since it enabled the composer to achieve coherence in works of some length which were not dancelike or fugal in character. The forms of *Passacaglia* and *Chaconne* employ the ground bass in combination with variation techniques, and sometimes transfer the bass melody to an upper part. Purcell, the greatest English composer of the seventeenth century, often uses the ground bass in his longer movements. In this example, the bass melody, which conforms to a descending chromatic type often found in ground basses, is three bars in length, a feature which avoids the squareness of the commoner four-bar bass, and gives the movement a flowing quality which is reinforced by causing the beginning of most repetitions of the bass to be overlapped by the unbroken melody of the upper part. The device used here by Purcell in the lower staff, that of making what is ostensibly a single melodic line produce upon the ear the effect of two parts, is often employed in Baroque keyboard writing. Bach employed the ground bass in a number of his finest movements, at times diversifying the key-scheme by allowing the bass to modulate—a device also used by Purcell. This composition originally occurred as a song, "Here the deities approve," in the *Ode for St. Cecilia's Day* of 1683, and was later published in *Orpheus Britannicus,* a collection of Purcell's music for solo voice. The present arrangement for keyboard instrument is thought to be the composer's own. The method of executing the ornaments is given above the notes the first time each ornament occurs.

Source: *The Second Part of Musick's Hand-Maid*, London, 1689.
    Modern edition: *The Works of Henry Purcell*, Vol. 6, London,
1895, pp. 30–31.

38. Henry Purcell (1659–1695)
Ground for Harpsichord, *A New Ground*

* Missing in original.

* Missing in original.

39. Arcangelo Corelli
Sonata da chiesa in E Minor, Op. 3, No. 7

The growth of instrumental ensemble music in the seventeenth century led to the creation of two important types of chamber music. The *sonata da camera* (chamber sonata), which was intended for domestic perform-ance, was a suite of dance-movements, similar to the keyboard suite.* The *sonata da chiesa* (church sonata) was more serious in tone than the *sonata da camera*, and usually employed a more polyphonic style, and made only a slight use of dance rhythms. It regularly consisted of four movements whose tempos were *slow, fast, slow, fast*. These separate movements, in differing tempos and meters, were developed from the earlier canzona, with its clearly contrasted but connected sections. Sonatas, both *da camera* and *da chiesa*, were composed for many differ-ent combinations of instruments, but the most universally popular com-bination was that of two violins with continuo. The resulting three printed lines of music (see the present example) gave rise to the term "trio sonata" to describe such compositions. This example, a typical *sonata da chiesa*, is the work of one of the greatest Italian composers of string music, Arcangelo Corelli, the Roman violinist and teacher of the late seventeenth and early eighteenth centuries, who is important for advances in violin technique as well as for his music. His solo and trio sonatas, as well as his concertos, were models for most late Baroque com-posers in these styles. As this example shows, the individual movements are distinguished by other features than their tempos. The first move-ment is usually in duple time, is majestic, and often makes a point of chains of suspensions. The second is most often fugal in style; the bass line takes part in the fugue at intervals, the violoncello being specifically

* The suite is discussed on p. 147.

saved, for the most part, to emphasize the entries of the subject, while the keyboard instrument supports the violins throughout. The third movement, often in triple time, is more lyrical than the first, while the final movement is dancelike, and often in two parts, with repeats, as are the dances of the suite. The writing for the strings, while not advanced in its technical demands, is distinctly stringlike, with no suggestion of vocal style. The continuo figuring is here left unrealized to facilitate study of the contrapuntal texture.

Source: *Sonate de chiesa a tre . . . da Arcangelo Corelli, Opera terza,* Modena, 1689, Sonata VII.
Modern edition: *Les Oeuvres de Arcangelo Corelli,* Book II, London, n.d., (c. 1885), p. 160.

39. Arcangelo Corelli (1653–1713)
Sonata da chiesa in E Minor, Op. 3, No. 7

40. François Couperin
Piece for Clavecin, *La Galante*

Following the bold and vigorous art of the virginalists, a new and sharply contrasting school of keyboard composers, the "clavecinists," arose in France about the middle of the seventeenth century. Its founder was Chambonnières, who took over many of the features of lute music in his graceful and refined pieces. The clavecinist style reached its climax in François Couperin, called "le Grand," whose works were greatly admired by Bach and Handel. A favorite musician of Louis XIV during the first part of the eighteenth century, Couperin cultivated the art of the miniature; his pieces have a polished, witty and elegant charm that reflects the *galanterie* of the court to which he was attached. This appropriately named example illustrates the pseudo-polyphony, free texture, and profusion of ornaments (*agréments*) which were Couperin's inheritance from the lutenists.* Nearly all his pieces bear descriptive titles, often so highly fanciful that there appears to be no relation between title and music. Most of his pieces are actually in the typical binary form of the suite movements, and can be readily identified as particular dances. For instance, *La Galante* is a gigue.

Source: F. Couperin, *Second livre de pièces de clavecin*, Paris, n.d., (?1717). Modern edition: F. Couperin, *Pièces de clavecin* (ed. J. Brahms & F. Chrysander), London, 1889, p. 217.

* The method of executing the ornaments in this piece is indicated above the notes, according to a table of ornaments and their interpretation furnished by the composer himself. It was a common practice of the period for composers to supply such tables.

40. François Couperin (1688–1759)
Piece for Clavecin, *La Galante*

41. Jean-Philippe Rameau
Scene from "Castor et Pollux," *Séjour de l'eternelle paix*

The powerful tradition of Lully's stylized opera dominated the French lyric stage long after his death. The Lully model was followed even by such an original figure as the great eighteenth-century French composer and theorist, Rameau. Like Lully, Rameau employed a "French" style of recitative in which the rhetorical rather than the musical is emphasized, the principal interest being in the rhythmic patterns, in contrast to the Italian *recitativo secco*.* As in the recitative section of the example given here, the meters of ¾, ¼, and ½ are freely alternated in an effort to reproduce musically the rhythms and inflections of the French language. In many important ways, however, Rameau was greatly superior to Lully, particularly in his expressive and dramatic use of harmony. Occupied throughout his life with the problems of musical theory, Rameau put into practice his ideas concerning the essential nature of music, based on the pre-eminence of harmony over melody. In his own words: "C'est l'harmonie qui nous guide, et non la mélodie" (Harmony is our guide, not melody). The scene given here is the one in which Castor, having been brought from the underworld to the Elysian fields and given immortality through the sacrificial act of his twin, is charmed by the beauty of the place, but troubled by the memory of his earthly love for Telaire, princess of Sparta. The mood of the scene is beautifully portrayed in the music; the instrumental prelude reflects the tranquil bliss of the heavenly abode, an effect which is heightened in Castor's lovely air, with

* For an illustration of *recitativo secco*, see p. 191 (Handel); the early recitative style appears on p. 126 (Monteverdi), and p. 130 (Carissimi).

its undercurrent of restlessness. The dormant conflict in his soul breaks forth in the impassioned recitative section, but subsides again in the *da capo*. The harmonic richness of the music is the greatest single element in the creation of the mood. Other characteristics of Rameau's style to be observed in the example are the economy of means whereby his effects are achieved, the sparing use of counterpoint, and the harmonic character of the melody. Aside from his harmonic resourcefulness, Rameau represents a great advance over Lully in his imaginative orchestration, a more extensive use of the chorus, and above all in the greater variety of instrumental music in his operas—overtures, descriptive "symphonies," and numerous dances. Nevertheless, Rameau's operas were the end of a long tradition; they were too overburdened with the conventions of a past epoch to live on as stage pieces. Attention is called to the fact that the example is transposed down a minor third, an indication of the cruel demands occasionally made by Rameau upon his singers.

Source: Rameau, *Castor et Pollux, tragédie mise en musique*, Paris, 1737. Modern edition: Jean-Philippe Rameau, *Oeuvres complètes*, Vol. VIII, Paris, 1903, p. 219.

41. Jean-Philippe Rameau (1683–1764)
Scene from "Castor et Pollux,"
Séjour de l'éternelle paix

[Original a minor 3rd higher]
Lent et gracieux

ne cal-mer-ez vous point____ mon âme im - pa - ti - en - te?
will you then nev-er calm____ my spi - rit so im - pa - tient?

Ne calm-er-ez vous point mon âme im - pa - ti - en____
Will you then nev-er calm my spi - rit so im - pa____

te?
tient?

Fin

Recitatif
Tem - ple des de - mi dieux que j'ha - bite à ja -
Tem - ple of all the gods, that I dwell in for

[Con.]

mais,   com - bat - tez   dans mon   coeur   ma flam - me   re - nais-
aye,   help me end   in my   heart   the fire   re - born with-

san - te! L'a - mour   jus - qu'en ces   lieux   me pour - suit   de   ses
in   me! For love   e'en to this   place   has pur - sued   with   his

traits: Cas - tor   n'y voit   que son   a - man - te,   et   vous per -
darts: and Cas - tor sees   on - ly   his   lov'd one,   and   you have

dez   tous vos   at - traits.   Sé-   te?
lost   all your   ap - peal.   A-   tient?

Que ce mur - mure_____ est
List to that mur_____mur

[Str. & Con.]

doux!_____ Que cet om - brage est frais!
sweet!_____ Mark how this shade is cool!

De ces ac - cords tou - chants la vo - lup - té m'en - chan - te, tout
Plea - sure is all a - round, all that I see en - chants me, all

rit,_____ tout pré - vient_____ mon at - ten - te,
smiles,_____ all re - strains_____ me from yearn - ing,

et   je forme en - cor_____ des re - grets!   Sé -
yet   I still am   seiz'd_____with re - grets!   A -

42. Domenico Scarlatti
Sonata in C Minor, for Harpsichord

One of the most strikingly original composers of the late Baroque period was Domenico Scarlatti, the Italian harpsichord virtuoso who was born in the same year as J. S. Bach, and who spent the greater part of his creative life at the Spanish court of Madrid. Scarlatti's fame chiefly rests upon a collection of more than five hundred keyboard compositions generally referred to as *sonatas*. The typical Scarlatti sonata is a movement in binary form, each part of which is marked to be repeated. Although Scarlatti's sonatas are not fully developed sonata movements such as those of the Viennese masters, certain of them represent an important stage in the evolution of sonata form. It should be noted that the only collection of these works published by Scarlatti himself is called *Essercizi per gravicembalo (Diversions for the Harpsichord)*, though each of the thirty individual pieces is labeled *sonata*. They exhibit a clarity of harmonic structure comparable to the work of Bach and Handel, together with an advanced type of keyboard writing which exerted a tremendous influence on the development of later piano music. Many of these movements are notable for their striking virtuosity, and make considerable technical demands on players even today. The present example shows some of the devices exploited by Scarlatti, such as the crossing of the left hand over the right, and the direct juxtaposition of brilliant scales with full chords. The almost complete absence of any pretense at polyphonic writing sets his music definitely apart from that of most of his late Baroque contemporaries. The version here given of this sonata reproduces accurately the simplicity and directness of the notation of the original edition.

Source: D. Scarlatti, *Essercizi per gravicembalo* (no place or date—c. 1746, possibly earlier; according to Burney, printed in Venice), Sonata XI, p. 33.

42. Domenico Scarlatti (1685–1757)
Sonata in C Minor, for Harpsichord

43. George Frederick Handel
Concerto Grosso in C Major, First Movement, for Oboes, Strings, and Continuo

---

The *concerto grosso* is the most important instrumental ensemble form of the Baroque period. The term *concerto*, used in the early Baroque period to describe any concerted music, especially that in which both instruments and voices participated, came later to be applied specifically to an instrumental form in which the essential principle is that of contrast between two instrumental groups. One of these is a large body, usually of strings, called variously the *tutti* (all), *concerto grosso* (large ensemble—the term which gave the name to the whole form), or *ripieno* (filling). The other is a much smaller group of individual players, called *solo*, or *concertino* (small ensemble). The contrast between these two bodies of players is established at the beginning of the typical concerto movement through the presentation by the tutti of a complete musical idea which returns at intervals during the subsequent course of the movement (hence its name, *ritornello*—"return"). After its first occurrence the solo passages become more numerous and the exchange between tutti and solo more rapid as the movement proceeds, and the whole is brought to a close by a presentation of the entire ritornello in the original key. The present example represents the mature development of the form: the ritornello is a passage of considerable length, opening with a striking figure that is easily identified on its recurrence, and closing with a solidly cadential passage also easily recognized on repetition. The solo group, made up of two violins and continuo, is that most frequently found in the concertos of Corelli and Vivaldi, and is the regular "trio sonata" combination of the Baroque. In this instance, Handel concludes the movement with a somewhat shortened version of the ritornello, which nevertheless preserves its individuality perfectly clearly. The later movements of the concerto are usually a slow movement and a concluding fast movement, in both of which the contrast between solo and tutti is less systematically carried out than in the first. The structural principle of the concerto is the basis for all late Baroque movements in which a contrast of forces is present. It is employed in the aria (see page 190), and is also the organizing principle of many movements for chorus and orchestra, especially those of Bach which are not strictly fugal. In a further development of the concerto grosso the solo group was reduced to a single instrument, usually the violin, which resulted in the solo concerto of Vivaldi and Bach.

Source: G. F. Handel, *Concerto per due violini concertini e violoncello, 2 hautb. 2 violini ripieno viola e basso,* in: *Select Harmony* (London, c.1741).
Modern edition: *Georg Friedrich Händels Werke* (Deutsche Händelgesellschaft), Vol. 21, Leipzig, 1865, p. 63.

43. George Frederick Handel (1685–1759)
Concerto Grosso in C Major, First Movement,
for Oboes, Strings, and Continuo

44. George Frederick Handel
Recitative, *Al valor del mio brando*, Sinfonia, and Aria, *Cara sposa*, from "Rinaldo"

By the end of the seventeenth century Italian opera had developed a clear distinction between passages of more or less straight declamation called *recitative*, where the words were the chief interest, and sections continuously lyrical and melodic called *aria*, in which the purely musical element was of primary importance. Recitative was of two sorts: that accompanied only by the continuo (*recitativo secco;* "dry recitative"), where the setting of the words closely approximated actual speech, with rhythmic and melodic interest at a minimum; and that accompanied by the orchestra (*recitativo accompagnato*), where rhythm was necessarily more regular and melody somewhat more developed. "Rinaldo" is the opera which established Handel as an operatic composer in London in 1711. It was based upon a scene from Tasso's *Gerusalemme liberata* (*Jerusalem Delivered*), a poem which furnished plots for numerous operas during the Baroque period, and even later. The *secco* recitative which begins the present example, a rapid interchange among three characters, occurs at that point in the opera where Armida, a sorceress, snatches the heroine Almirena from the arms of the hero Rinaldo. During the instrumental *sinfonia* which follows, Rinaldo draws his sword in an attempt to rescue his beloved, but a dark cloud filled with horrible monsters descends upon Armida and Almirena, and they vanish. This short movement for orchestra is typical of the manner in which instrumental interludes were employed in the Italian opera of this period to enhance stage action, a practice also encountered in French opera of the same time. This is a use of the orchestra whose earliest beginnings can be found in

Monteverdi. The simple but effective string writing is very characteristic of Handel. Left desolate, Rinaldo expresses his grief in the aria which follows. The form of the *da capo aria* was brought to full maturity in the works of Alessandro Scarlatti, the composer upon whose work Handel, during his years in Italy, modeled his operatic style. In this form, a complete first section is followed by a lengthy middle section, usually in a contrasting key and style, the first section then being repeated entire (*da capo*, "from the head"), thus producing an *aba* plan. The structural principal of the first section in itself is based upon the contrast between the opening ritornello * presented by the accompaniment at the beginning, and the entries of the solo voice. These are set off by recurrences of the ritornello material, with the ritornello closing the whole, a procedure precisely similar to that employed in the concerto grosso. Many mature arias by Bach and others lack the distinct middle section and the *da capo* of the opening, but all are built upon the ritornello plan. *Cara sposa* is an example of the "pathetic" style of aria. The decided contrast in style and tempo presented by the middle section is somewhat uncommon, and even approaches accompanied recitative in the vigor of its declamation and the quick interjections of the orchestra. The text of the main section of the aria was usually, as here, very brief, so that the lengthy musical form required much repetition of words. It is interesting to note that in the Italian operatic style it was customary for the singer to add improvised embellishments (*fioriture*) to the original simple melodic line, especially during the *da capo*. Handel told Sir John Hawkins, the eminent musical historian, that he considered *Cara sposa* one of the two finest songs he had ever written, the other being *Ombra cara* from "Radamisto." The beauty and finish of the string writing in this aria is particularly noteworthy. Concerning the unfigured continuo, see page 129.

Source: *Georg Friedrich Händels Werke* (Deutsche Händelgesellschaft), Vol. 58, Leipzig, 1896, p. 38.

* The ritornello is explained on p. 182.

44. George Frederick Handel (1685–1759)
Recitative, *Al valor del mio brando,*
Sinfonia, and Aria, *Cara sposa,* from "Rinaldo"

Armida

des - se il To - nan - te.   Tan - to_ar - di - sci_ar - ro - gan - te?
Jove should de - mand her.   Art so dar - ing, O vain one?

Presto [Ob I—Vln I]

[Con.]   [Ob II—Vln II]   [Vla]

[Con.]

(tr)

Rinaldo

Ca_____ra
Wife_____be-

spo - sa, a - man - te ca - ra, do - ve
lov - ed. dear - est of wo - men, pray, where

se - i?_____ do - ve se - i? Deh! ri-
art thou?_____ pray, where art thou? Ah! re-

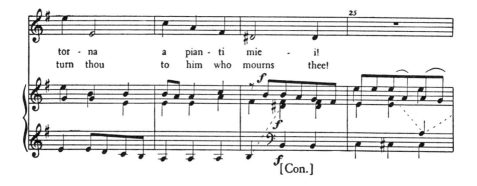

tor - na a pian - ti mie - i!
turn thou to him who mourns thee!

[Con.]

tor - na!   deh!   ri - tor - na a pian___ti___ mie -
turn thou!   ah!   re - turn   thou to___ him who mourns

i! ca - ra spo - sa,   spo - sa ca - ra,
thee! wife be - lov - ed,   dear - est wife thou,

do - ve se - i?   deh!___ ri___
pray, where art thou?   ah!___ re___

tor - na,   do - ve sei, do - ve sei? deh! ri -
turn thou,   pray where art thou, where art thou, re -

Fine

Allegro

Del vo - stro E - re - bo sull'____ a - ra   col - la fa - ce   del mio
From your mon - arch E - re - bus hi - ther   I de - fy you,   with the

sde - gno   io vi sfi - do,   col - la   fa - ce del mio sde - gno io vi sfi - do,   O___
flam - ing   of my an - ger,   with the flam - ing of   my an - ger I de - fy you,   O___

spir___ti___ re - i!   Col - la fa___ce   del___ mio sde - gno, del vo-
spir___its of dark - ness!   With the flam___ing   of___ my an - ger, from your

[Con.]   [Str.]

stro E - re___bo___ sull' a___ra,   io vi sfi - do,   io vi sfi - do,   O___
mon - arch___ E___ re - bus hi___ther,   I de - fy' you,   I de - fy you,   O___

90   (tr)   Da Capo

spir___ti___ re - i,   O___ spir___ti___ re___i!
spir___its of dark - ness,   O___ spir___its of dark___ness!

[Con.]

45. George Frederick Handel
Chorus, *Draw the Tear from Hopeless Love,* from "Solomon"

The Baroque *oratorio*, which reached its perfection in the work of Handel, employed the same forms as the opera of the period, but the chorus, which in the opera played but an insignificant role, became in the oratorio the chief agent of the drama. Handel's choruses are justly regarded as the final proof of his greatness as a composer. Unlike Bach's choral movements, they are almost never constructed on a ritornello, or on a strictly fugal plan. Instead, they exhibit the utmost freedom of form, following the sense of the text from point to point with complete fidelity, and employ imitative or chordal texture in quick alternation. This chorus from "Solomon" shows all these points very clearly. It occurs in the oratorio as one of a series of choruses presented as entertainment for the Queen of Sheba on her visit to Solomon, as related in I Kings 10:1–13. The subject of this entertainment is the power of music to move the spirit of man, and this chorus deals with the emotion of hopeless love, "full of death and wild despair." The opening fugal exposition, with its intensely powerful subject, and the setting of the whole text, is an example of Handel's mastery of expressive musical rhetoric. The orchestration is of unusual subtlety for Handel, who is sometimes rather perfunctory in his scoring. Throughout the chorus, the leading players in each section of the string orchestra sustain the background harmonies, contributing a violent urgency to the middle section by their reiterated chords in dotted rhythm, while the voices are doubled first by oboes and bassoons, and from bar 10 by the ripieno strings. The close shows Handel's fine use of expressive harmonies for dramatic effect. The continuo figuring is rather sparse, as is usual with Handel.

Source: *Georg Friedrich Händels Werke* (Deutsche Händelgesellschaft) Vol. 26, Leipzig, 1867, p. 240.

45. George Frederick Handel (1685–1759)
Chorus, *Draw the Tear from Hopeless Love,*
from "Solomon"

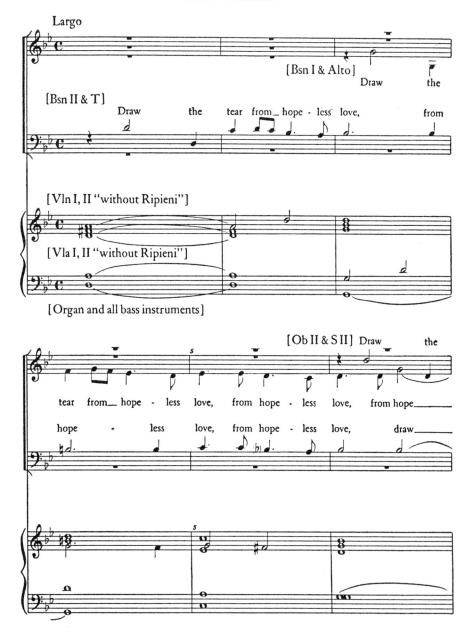

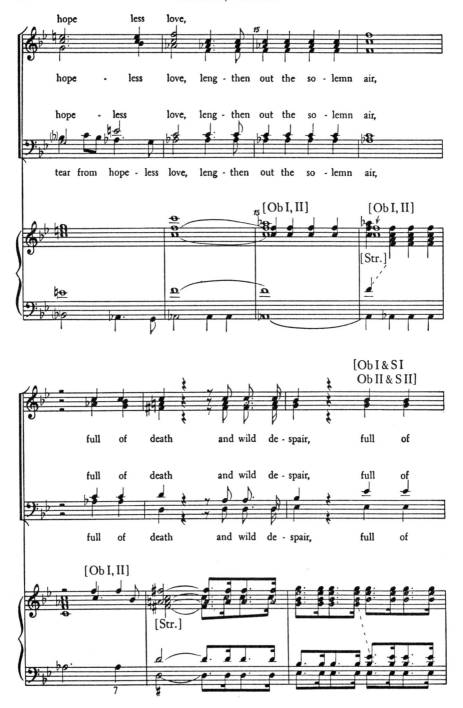

46. Johann Sebastian Bach
Chorale, *Christ lag in Todesbanden,* from Cantata No. 4

The term *chorale* is applied to the hymn tunes of the Lutheran Church. The use of such vernacular hymns, already rather common before the Reformation, was actively fostered by Martin Luther, who, with his assistants, drew upon Catholic hymns and secular songs for texts and melodies to furnish a repertory of congregational music. The great body of sacred melody and poetry thus created served throughout the whole Baroque period as the basis for two of the most important categories of German Protestant musical composition: the church *cantata,** and the organ *chorale prelude* (Example 47, page 214). Of the long line of composers who occupied themselves with the chorale, Bach is unquestionably the greatest. The melody of this chorale is a revision by Luther's colleague, Johann Walther, of a still older melody, which was itself probably based upon plain song. The words of the Easter hymn to which the tune belongs are by Luther himself. The typical chorale melody, as here illustrated, is divided into lines corresponding to the lines of the text, the final note of each line being customarily marked by a fermata. Bach's harmonization of the chorale shows his great mastery of a simple yet powerful part-writing, each voice being given an expressive line of its own, and the whole being perfectly calculated as an expression of the traditional melody and words. The present four-part version of the chorale is the final movement of Bach's Church Cantata No. 4, every movement of which is based upon this melody. It is here given with the text of the first verse; that of the final (seventh) verse, to which it is sung in the

---

* The plan of the German church cantata is described on p. 215.

Cantata, is given below. A chorus from the same cantata is given in Example 48. As is usual in a simple chorale which closes a cantata, all the instruments employed in the preceding movements double whatever voice part is convenient for their range.

Source: *Johann Sebastian Bachs Werke* (Bach-Gesellschaft), Vol. I, Leipzig, 1851, p. 124.

Text of seventh stanza:

> *Wir essen und leben wohl*
> *Im rechten Osterfladen,*
> *Der alte Sauerteig nicht soll*
> *Sein bei dem Wort der Gnaden,*
> *Christus will die Koste sein*
> *Und speisen die Seel' allein,*
> *Der Glaub' will keins andern leben.*
> *Hallelujah!*

> We celebrate this Holy Feast
> In reverence united.
> The evil leaven works no more;
> Thy Word its curse has righted.
> Christ's own self the feast shall be
> And nourish our souls, that we
> By faith may gain salvation.
> Hallelujah!

English text by Henry S. Drinker

46. Johann Sebastian Bach (1685–1750)
Chorale, *Christ lag in Todesbanden,*
from Cantata No. 4

sing - en____ Hal_____le_____lu_____jah.
sing we____ Hal_____le_____lu_____jah.

Hal_____le - lu - jah!

Hal_____le_____lu - jah!
Hal_____le_____lu____jah!

Hal_____le_____lu_____jah!

47. Johann Sebastian Bach
Chorale Prelude for Organ, *Christ lag in Todesbanden*

The *chorale prelude*, like the fugue, is a form which was practiced throughout the Baroque period and brought to perfection by Bach. The origin of this form lay in its use as an introduction to the congregational singing of the hymn-tune, but in its mature manifestations it formed an important type of composition, often of considerable length, whose function was to set the mood of the service and to form a poetic musical commentary on the original hymn-text. The chorale prelude was extensively cultivated by Bach's North German predecessors—notably Scheidt, Buxtehude, Pachelbel and Böhm. A large number of chorale prelude types was practiced by Bach. The most important of these were: the *motet*—a treatment of the chorale line by line as a series of fugal expositions; the *ornamented*—an elaborate "coloring" of the melody, with free accompanying parts; the *partita*—a set of variations on the chorale; the *canonic*—a treatment of the chorale in canon, with figuration in the other voices; the *figured*—in which the chorale is presented continuously as a *cantus firmus* (usually in the soprano), the other voices consisting of characteristic motives treated in free polyphony. *Christ lag in Todesbanden* (Christ Lay in the Bonds of Death) is an example of the last-named type, in which Bach modeled his style on that of Pachelbel. The intimate, poetic, mystic feeling with which it is suffused is characteristic of Bach's ability to embody in his settings the feeling present in the hymn with which the tune is associated. This chorale prelude comes from a collection of such pieces, the *Orgelbüchlein* (*Little Organ Book*), which was planned by Bach to include settings of chorales for

all the festivals of the Church year. However, only those parts of the plan
which dealt with the greater festivals were fully executed.

Source: *Johann Sebastian Bachs Werke*, (Bach-Gesellschaft), Vol. 25, 2,
Leipzig, 1878, p. 38.

47. Johann Sebastian Bach (1685–1750)
Chorale Prelude for Organ,
Christ lag in Todesbanden

48. Johann Sebastian Bach

Chorus, *Es war ein wunderlicher Krieg*, from Cantata No. 4

This is the fourth movement of Bach's Church Cantata No. 4, a work based throughout upon Luther's chorale, *Christ lag in Todesbanden*, each of whose seven verses is used as the text for a separate movement. (For the text of the first and final verses, and for the simple chorale in four-part setting as it appears in the final movement of the cantata, see pages 209–211.) The church cantata as Bach practiced it was a combination of essentially German elements, derived from the seventeenth-century development begun by Schütz, with the forms and types of the Italian opera. Thus most of Bach's cantatas open with a chorus, usually constructed on a ritornello, and followed by a series of recitatives and arias, with the additional element of the German chorale, which may be employed in any of the previous movements, and which usually concludes the cantata. The present example is not a ritornello movement, but is a *chorale motet*, so called because the text is treated line by line as in the sixteenth-century motet. An added feature of the chorale motet is the fact that the material for all the voices is derived from the chorale melody itself, each of whose lines is made the basis for a fugal exposition in which the final entry is the unadorned chorale melody in long notes. This augmentation of the melody is usually given to the top voice; here it is, exceptionally, assigned to the alto. The present movement is accompanied only by the continuo, in deliberate contrast to the adjacent movements in the cantata. The continuo line itself, to facilitate study, has been omitted from this example. When the vocal bass is present, the continuo is usually identical with it, with minor melodic variations, the nature of which can be seen in the detailed version of bars 5 and 6 given at the end of the example. When the bass voice is silent, the continuo is identical with the lowest sounding part. It should be noted that since the continuo line is always assumed to be doubled at an octave below the written notes, the crossing of the vocal bass above the tenor does not alter the fact that the bass furnishes the foundation of the harmony (see the small notes in bars 15, 25, and 26). Exceptionally, in bars 30–31 and 34–35, the continuo differs from all the vocal parts, and is accordingly set out on a separate stave.

English text adapted from Henry S. Drinker.

Source: *Johann Sebastian Bachs Werke*, (Bach-Gesellschaft) Vol. 1, Leipzig, 1851, p. 114.

Biblical references:
"Then shall be brought to pass the saying that is written that Death is swallowed up in victory. O grave, where is thy victory?" I Cor. 15:54.
"He will swallow up death in victory." Isaiah 25:8.

48. Johann Sebastian Bach (1685–1750)
Chorus, *Es war ein wunderlicher Krieg,*
from Cantata No. 4

da Tod und Le - ben run_____
with Death and Life em - bat_____

Es war ein wun - der - lich - er Krieg, ein wun_____der - lich - er
It was a won - der - ful ar - ray, a won_____der - ful ar -

[Continuo in unison with lowest sounding voice—see notes]

gen, es war ein wun - der - lich - er Krieg, da Tod und Le - ben run_____
tled, it was a won - der - ful ar - ray, with Death and Life em - bat_____

Krieg, da Tod und Le - ben run_____gen, da Tod und Le - ben run_____
ray, with Death and Life em - bat_____tled, with Death and Life em - bat_____

Es war ein wun - der - lich - er Krieg, ein wun_____der - lich - er
It was a won - der - ful ar - ray, a won_____der - ful ar -

gen, ein wun - der - lich - er Krieg,   es war ein wun - der - lich - er
tled, a won - der - ful ar - ray,   it was a won - der - ful ar -

Es   war   ein   wun - der - lich - er
It   was   a   won - der - ful ar -

gen, es war ein wun - der - lich - er Krieg, es war ein wun - der - lich - er
tled it was a won - der - ful ar - ray, it was a won - der - ful ar -

Krieg, da Tod und Le - ben run_____gen, es war ein wun - der - lich - er
ray, with Death and Life em - bat_____tled, it was a won - der - ful ar -

hat ver - kün di - get das, ver - kün di - get
say - ing, writ ten thus will come to
Die Schrift hat ver - kün di - get
So will come to pass the say
kün di - get das, ver - kün di - get
comes to pass, comes to pass the say -
das, die Schrift hat ver - kün di - get, ver -
pass, so the say - ing comes to pass, the
Die Schrift hat ver - kün - digt das,
So the say - ing comes to pass,
das, die Schrift hat ver - kün
ing, so the say - ing comes
das, die Schrift hat ver - kün
ing, so will come to pass
kün - di - get das, wie ein Tod den an - dern frass, wie ein Tod
say - ing writ - ten, that Death will be swal - lowed up, that Death will
di - get das, wie ein Tod den an - dern frass, wie
to pass, that Death will be swal-lowed up, that
di - get das, wie ein Tod den an - dern
the say - ing, that Death will be swal - lowed
[Con.]

Bars 5 and 6, showing variations between the vocal Bass and the Continuo

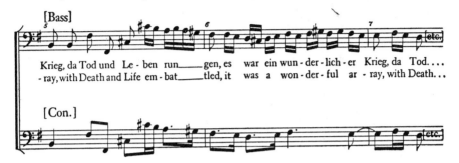

Krieg, da Tod und Le - ben run____gen, es   war ein wun - der - lich - er Krieg, da Tod....
- ray, with Death and Life em - bat____tled, it   was a   won - der - ful ar - ray, with Death...

49. Johann Sebastian Bach
Arioso for Alto, *Ach Golgatha,* from the
"St. Matthew Passion"

The *Passion* was a musical treatment of the events in the life of Christ from the triumphal entry into Jerusalem on Palm Sunday to the Crucifixion. The earliest Passions were composed in the fifteenth century, but during the Baroque period compositions of this type became a highly important special form of oratorio. Two such works of Bach are preserved, one according to the Gospel of St. John, and one according to St. Matthew, the latter being generally regarded as one of the greatest masterpieces of all time. The present example, designated "recitative" in the score of the "St. Matthew Passion," is in *arioso* style, midway between true recitative, with its free rhythm and syllabic diction, and aria, with its steady rhythm and elaborated melody. The rhythm here is perfectly strict, but the vocal part is of the sort usual in recitative, almost entirely syllabic, and preoccupied not with melody as such but with the most exact expression of the words. In this meditation on the hill called Golgatha, upon which the Crucifixion took place, Bach exhibits his powers as a tone-poet at their highest and most moving. As is his usual practice in such movements, he adopts a melodic, harmonic, and rhythmic pattern for the accompaniment which remains unchanged throughout the arioso. The instrumentation is particularly fine, with the dark color of the *oboe da caccia* (a tenor oboe), the *ostinato* of the *pizzicato* cellos (here liberated from their usual continuo function), and the unvarying pulsation of the continuo. Against this orchestral background the alto voice declaims a text whose every detail Bach follows with the utmost fidelity. Not only does his tone-painting deal vividly with such words as "verderben" (perish), "Kreuz" (cross), and "sterben" (die), but he can set "Himmel" (heaven) and "Luft" (air) to high notes, and "Erde" (earth) to a low one, without in any way breaking the deeply moving atmosphere of the whole.

English text by Henry S. Drinker

Source: *Johann Sebastian Bachs Werke* (Bach-Gesellschaft) Vol. 4, Durchgesehene Ausgabe (ed. Max Schneider), Leipzig, 1935, p. 233.

Note: The final bar, almost universally misprinted with only a whole note *a*-flat in the continuo, was intended by Bach as here given. For the circumstances leading to the mistaken version, see the above-cited revision of Volume 4 of the Bach-Gesellschaft edition, p. xix.

49. Johann Sebastian Bach (1685–1750)
Arioso for Alto, *Ach Golgatha,*
from the "St. Matthew Passion"

Alto

Ach Gol - ga -tha,   un - sel' - ges Gol - ga - tha!
Ah Gol - go -tha,   ac - cur - sed Gol - go - tha!

[Oboe da caccia I, II]

[Vc. pizz]

[Con.]

Der Herr der Herr -lich - keit muss schimpf-lich hier ver - der_____ben,
The Lord of Glo - ry they in shame are cru - ci - fy_____ing;

der Se - gen und das Heil der Welt wird als ein Fluch an's Kreuz ge-
the Blest Re-deem - er of Man - kind is spat on, tor - tured and ma -

stellt.
ligned.

Dem Schö - pfer Him - mels und der Er - den soll
Of earth and sky, from Him de - riv - ed, will

Erd'___ und Luft ent - zo - gen wer - den; die Un - schuld
He___ who made them be de - priv - ed; the Sin - less

muss hier schul - dig ster - ben; das ge - het mei - ner See - le
now for sin is dy - ing; and so no cheer my soul may

nah; Ach Gol - ga - tha, un - sel' - ges Gol - ga - tha!
find. Ah Gol - go - tha, ac - curs - ed Gol - go - tha!

50. Johann Sebastian Bach
Fugue, *Contrapunctus III*, from "Die Kunst der Fuge"

Bach's life-long interest in the problems of fugue writing, which made him unquestionably the greatest master of this style who ever lived, culminated in the series of nineteen fugues and canons based on the same subject which is known as "Die Kunst der Fuge" ("The Art of Fugue"). In this work, left incomplete at his death, a single subject is employed in an extraordinary variety of fugue styles, resulting in an unparalleled demonstration of technical mastery and inexhaustible musical inventiveness. While the original edition gives no indication of the medium for which these compositions were conceived, since they are presented in open score, with each voice on a separate stave, internal evidence makes it reasonably clear that they are for keyboard. The *subject* upon which all the fugues and canons of "The Art of Fugue" are based is shown at the end of the example. In the present example, the third fugue of the series, each of which is called *contrapunctus* (counterpoint), the subject has been inverted, and actually is first presented in what would normally be its *answer* form. The *countersubject* (bars 5–8) begins chromatically, and its regular appearances with each entry of the subject give a chromatic character to the whole composition. The first *episode* (bars 19–22) is derived from the countersubject, and makes use of symmetrical interchange of motives between the two upper voices. The next entry of the subject (soprano, bars 23–26) is varied by the use of passing tones and syncopations, a device seldom encountered elsewhere in fugue literature, including Bach's own fugues. After the second episode (bars 27–28) the same varied form of the subject appears in the tenor (bars 29–32) and after the third episode (bars 33–34) once more in the same voice (bars 35–38). This last-mentioned entry is not accompanied by the counter-subject. After the fourth episode (bars 39–42), which is a further treatment of the material which formed the first episode, the subject in its original unvaried form occurs in the soprano (bars 43–46), followed by a fifth episode (bars 47–50). A series of subject entries not separated by episodes follows. The first (bass, bars 51–54) presents the unvaried subject, while the second and third (alto and soprano, bars 55–61) have the passing tones of the varied form, but not the syncopation. The last two entries overlap by one bar, and are thus technically in *stretto* (a close imitation of the subject in which the answer begins before the subject is completed). The final statement of the subject is in the unvaried form (tenor, bars 63–66), and this is followed by a close of six bars. The fugue is here arranged on two staves, with suggestions for the solo performer as to the distribution of the parts between the hands where this is not easily perceived.

Source: *Johann Sebastian Bachs Werke* (Bach-Gesellschaft), Vol. 25, 1, Leipzig, 1878, p. 10, ed. W. Rust.
("Die Kunst der Fuge" was re-edited by W. Graeser in Vol. 47, Leipzig, 1926.)

50. Johann Sebastian Bach (1685–1750)
Fugue, *Contrapunctus III*, from "Die Kunst der Fuge"

Subject of "The Art of Fugue"